SMART MONEY SKILLS FOR TEENS: THE ULTIMATE SOURCE FOR FINANCIAL FREEDOM

FROM BUDGETS TO INVESTING, LEVERAGING AI FOR MONEY AND TIME MANAGEMENT TO ACCELERATE SUCCESS

RENO SMITH

TABLE OF CONTENTS

INTRODUCTION

Ever had that moment when you open your wallet and all you find is a library card and maybe your driver's license? We've all been there. Money doesn't grow on trees, but it sure disappears faster than a Snapchat story. I have a saying that sums it up:

"Money is like magic. Now you see it, now you don't. Poof! And it's gone."

The only way to stop money from vanishing is to take control of it. And there's no better time than now, while you're young. Believe it or not, how you handle money today will shape your entire future.

This book, **Smart Money Skills for Teens: The Ultimate Source for Financial Freedom**, is your guide to navigating the tricky world of budgeting, saving, and investing—with a little help from AI tools. Think of it as your money GPS, steering you through the twists and turns of personal finance. Whether you're saving up for the latest gaming console, a date, college, or even your first car, this book has got you covered.

Why is this book important? Well, let's face it: schools don't always teach us how to manage money. Yet, it's one of the most important skills you'll ever learn. This book breaks it down into bite-sized, easy-to-understand pieces. No boring lectures here—just practical advice you can start using right away.

So, who is this book for? If you're a teen figuring out how to manage your allowance or your first paycheck, this book is for you. If you're a parent wanting to help your child develop healthy financial habits, you're in the right place too. This book is designed to be an engaging, supportive guide for teens, young adults, and their supportive parents.

Now, a little about me: I'm a lawyer, former soldier, entrepreneur, and senior global business executive. Over the years, I've learned—sometimes the hard way—that managing money is a crucial skill. I'm passionate about helping teens (and supportive parents) overcome financial challenges and achieve independence. I've seen too many young people (my younger self included) struggle with money simply because they didn't have the right tools or knowledge. That's why I wrote this book: to make personal finance accessible—and even fun.

The structure of this book is straightforward. We'll start with the basics: understanding money and creating a budget. Then we'll dive into saving, because who doesn't want a little extra cash for emergencies or fun stuff? After that, we'll explore investing, so you can make your money work for you. Finally, we'll wrap up with tips for staying financially healthy in the long run.

Expect to learn practical skills you can use right away. You'll find answers to questions you didn't even know you had—and maybe even a few laughs along the way. Managing money doesn't have to be boring! Most importantly, expect to feel more confident about your financial future.

There is a workbook available online, and there's a bonus chapter at the end of the book on AI and how it can help you execute everything you've learned. Think of it as your secret weapon for speeding up your financial journey. My strong advice: just glance at it for now. Focus on the basics first. AI is a tool to leverage once you've built a solid foundation.

Managing money can seem overwhelming, but you can do it. This book is here to help every step of the way. By the end, you'll have a solid understanding of personal finance and feel ready to take control of your financial future. It's not about being perfect; it's about making smart choices and learning from your mistakes.

So, are you ready to become a money management pro? Let's get started!

CHAPTER 1
UNDERSTANDING THE BASICS AND MINDSET

> "It's not about how much money you make, but how much money you keep, how hard it works for you, and how many generations you keep it for."
>
> ROBERT KIYOSAKI

E ver found yourself staring at your empty wallet, wondering where all your money went? "Poof!" Maybe you bought that shiny new gadget or splurged on a night out with friends. We've all been there, and it's totally normal. But here's the thing: understanding how to manage your money now can save you from a lot of headaches later. This chapter is all about getting the basics down and developing the right financial mindset. We'll explore why financial literacy is crucial, how it impacts your future, and what it means for your overall well-being. Trust me, this stuff is way more important than you might think.

1.1 WHY FINANCIAL LITERACY MATTERS FOR TEENS

First, let's talk about why learning to manage money is so important. Picture your future self living in your dream apartment, driving a sweet car, or maybe even running your own business. All these dreams require one thing: money. But it's not just about having money; it's about knowing how to manage it. Financial literacy sets the stage for independence and responsibility. By understanding budgeting, saving, and investing, you gain control over your financial future. You won't need to rely on anyone to bail you out.

Avoiding common financial pitfalls is another reason financial literacy matters. Many adults struggle with debt, overspending, and poor credit scores because they didn't learn how to manage money when they were younger. By learning these skills now, you can avoid these traps. Imagine not having to worry about credit card debt or scrambling to make ends meet. Building good habits, like saving a portion of your allowance or paycheck, will make your financial journey much smoother.

Financial literacy also plays a huge role in achieving your life goals. Want to go to college without drowning in student loans? Knowing how to save and apply for scholarships can make that happen. Dreaming of buying your first car? Budgeting and saving can turn that dream into reality. Financial literacy is like a secret weapon that helps you turn your dreams into plans.

But it's not just about money. Financial stability impacts your overall well-being. When you're in control of your finances, you're free to focus on important things like your studies, hobbies, and relationships. Being financially literate gives you the confidence to tackle challenges and seize opportunities without constantly worrying about money.

Let's look at some real-life examples. Noah Booth, a teen, wrote *A Rich Future: Essential Financial Concepts for Youth*. He started investing his savings at age 10 and realized there were few resources on personal finance for teens. His early start has given him a significant advantage. Then there's John Rogers, Jr. His parents gave him stocks instead of Christmas gifts when he was young, so he began managing money and stocks early. Today, he's the Chairman of Ariel Capital Management, which manages billions for clients.

These examples show that financial literacy is a powerful tool that opens doors to amazing opportunities. So, buckle up and get ready to dive into the world of financial literacy. Your future self will thank you!

1.2 MONEY 101: BASIC FINANCIAL TERMS YOU NEED TO KNOW

Now, let's break down some financial basics. You've probably heard terms like "budget," "savings," and "interest" thrown around by adults, but they're not as mysterious as they seem.

Budget: Think of a budget as a roadmap for your money. If you're planning a road trip, you wouldn't just drive aimlessly—you'd plan your route, know where to stop for gas, and figure out where you'll stay. A budget helps you track how much money is coming in (from allowance or a part-time job) and how much is going out (for snacks, video games, or that streaming subscription). A budget keeps you from running out of money, just like planning a route keeps you from running out of gas.

Savings: Savings are money you set aside for future use—a safety net. It's like a squirrel storing nuts for the winter. Whether you're saving for a new phone or college, having savings means you're prepared for whatever comes your way.

Interest: Interest is either a reward for saving money or a fee for borrowing it. Let's say you put your savings in a bank account. The bank uses your money to make loans and, in return, pays you a little extra—this is interest. It's like planting a tree and getting fruit in return. The longer you leave your money in, the more fruit (interest) you get. On the flip side, if you borrow money, you must pay interest, like renting a bike and paying a fee for using it.

To bring this to life: Suppose you get a $50 monthly allowance. You budget $10 for snacks, $15 for entertainment, $10 for savings, and $15 for other expenses. Sticking to this plan ensures you won't run out of money. Now, if you save $10 a month, by the end of the year, you'll have $120. And if you put that $120 into a bank account earning 2% interest, at the end of the year, you'll have $122.40. Over time, this adds up!

Quick Glossary:

- **Budget:** A plan for spending and saving money.
- **Savings:** Money set aside for future use.
- **Interest:** A reward for saving or a fee for borrowing money.

Understanding these terms is like learning the ABCs of personal finance. Once you get the hang of them, managing your money becomes a lot less intimidating—and even empowering.

1.3 SETTING THE STAGE: YOUR FINANCIAL GOALS

Let's talk goals. Whether it's buying a new bike, going to a concert, or saving for college, you need a plan to turn those dreams into reality. That's where **SMART goals** come in. SMART stands for Specific, Measurable, Achievable, Relevant, and Time-Bound.

For example, say you want to save $500 for a new bike. The goal is **Specific** (you know exactly what you're saving for). It's **Measurable** (you can track your progress). It's **Achievable** (saving $500 is within reach). It's **Relevant** (a bike will give you freedom and mobility). And it's **Time-Bound** (you set a six-month deadline to reach your goal).

Now, let's look at **short-term** and **long-term** goals. Short-term goals can be achieved relatively quickly, like saving for a concert next month. Long-term goals, like saving for college or a car, take more time and consistent effort.

A **Financial Action Plan** is like your roadmap. First, identify your goal. Next, create a timeline and break it down into smaller steps. For example, if you want to save $1,000 for a summer trip, aim to save $100 a month. Tracking your progress will keep you motivated.

Start with small, achievable goals, like saving for a concert. As you master this process, you'll be ready for bigger goals like college or starting a business. Write down your goals, track your progress, and stay focused.

1.4 THE FINANCIAL MINDSET: ATTITUDES TOWARD MONEY

Money isn't just paper, coins, or numbers on a screen—it's a tool. And like any tool, it can either help you build the life you want or become a source of stress. The key to using money effectively lies in your mindset.

Viewing money as a tool means recognizing it as a means to an end, not an end in itself. When you see money this way, you understand its power to create opportunities, whether that's furthering your education, starting a business, or treating yourself to something special. This mindset helps you make decisions that align with your goals, rather than getting caught in a cycle of spending and regretting.

Years ago, I wrote a note to my children about what I learned about money through both good and tough experiences. Here's what I said:

"I'm sending these thoughts for your consideration, reflecting my experience and external advice (most of which I wish I had followed at the time). Hint, hint.

This first one is about MONEY:

1. Money is like magic; if you don't watch it, it will just go "Poof" and disappear! I assume you've already experienced this.
2. *Don't negotiate for dollars; negotiate for opportunity.* This was the advice of a wise and successful businessman. And he was wrong. Go for the money. It's your security blanket and provides flexibility.
3. *A job is for a paycheck and does not determine your self-worth.* Your grandad told your mom and me this when we were newly married, and we only learned the lesson late in our careers. Do your work for the money so that you can live the life you want. Your career shouldn't define you

completely—it's how you live outside of work that brings real joy. Career success matters, but I found it's secondary to living a fulfilled life.

4. *Pay your bills on time, avoid using credit if possible, and if you must, pay it off quickly.* And above all: Save, Save, Save. I learned these lessons the hard way. Don't repeat my mistakes. Your mom and I are much better now because we figured these things out.

5. *Money can buy happiness.* Or at least, it makes happiness more likely. Anyone who says otherwise is "misinformed."

If you don't follow these five points, you'll be stressed, limited in what you can do, and constantly struggling to fix the money problems you created. Please, take these lessons to heart, master your personal finances, and your life will be much easier."

I share these insights because I'm passionate about your success. Your parents might have different views, but I hope this book opens up opportunities for you to sit down together, discuss money, and create financial alignment as a family. Now, back to work!

Next up: **Frugality**. Embracing frugality doesn't mean being stingy or never having fun. It's about making thoughtful choices and getting the most value from your money. Frugality teaches you to prioritize what truly matters and avoid wasting money on things that don't add real value to your life. It's the difference between buying overpriced tech or finding a high-quality, gently used one that does the job just as well. Mastering frugality early on can lead to a lifetime of smart financial decisions.

Let's talk about **financial self-discipline**—this is where the rubber meets the road. Self-discipline in financial decisions means having the control to avoid impulse buys. Picture this: you're at the mall, and you spot a pair of Jordans you love. They're not in your budget, but the temptation is real. Financial self-discipline helps you walk away, knowing that protecting your financial future is more important than a momentary thrill. It's also about delaying gratification. Instead of blowing your birthday money on video games, you could save it for a more meaningful purchase later, like a more powerful (gaming) laptop "for school."

Developing a **growth mindset about money** is essential for long-term success. This means viewing challenges as learning opportunities, not roadblocks. Made a financial mistake? No worries—consider it a lesson. Spent too much on fast food and didn't have enough for something else? Adjust your budget and move forward. The more financial education you seek, the better equipped you'll be to make smart decisions. Read books, watch videos, and talk to knowledgeable people. The internet is full of resources—take advantage of them!

Take this example: a teen wanted to buy a high-end camera for photography. Instead of splurging right away, he saved diligently over several months, cutting back on unnecessary expenses and picking up odd jobs. His patience paid off—he got the camera and ingrained valuable financial habits in the process. Another story is of an adult who reflects on her disciplined teen years, where saving and budgeting allowed her to graduate college debt-free and buy her first home in her twenties. That early self-discipline gave her a significant head start in life.

Adopting a positive financial mindset, embracing frugality, and developing self-discipline will transform the way you handle money. It's about making smart choices that align with your goals and learning from every experience. With these strategies, you'll build a strong financial foundation that will serve you well for life. The journey may have challenges, but the rewards are worth it.

1.5 NEEDS VS. WANTS: MAKING SMART SPENDING DECISIONS

Let's be real—we've all been there. You're standing in a store, holding something shiny and new, wondering, *"Do I really need this?"* Sometimes, it's hard to tell. That's where understanding the difference between needs and wants becomes crucial.

Needs are the essentials—things you can't live without, like food, clothing, and shelter. These basics keep you alive and healthy. **Wants** are the fun extras—video games, designer shoes, or that daily iced latte from your favorite coffee shop. While wants can make life more enjoyable, they're not necessary for survival.

So, why does this distinction matter? Because constantly splurging on wants while ignoring your needs can lead to financial chaos. Imagine spending all your money on the latest tech, only to realize you don't have enough left for school supplies. It's like eating dessert before dinner and being too full to enjoy the main course. Prioritizing your needs ensures you cover the essentials first, allowing you to enjoy your wants guilt-free when you can afford them.

Here's a simple framework for making smart spending decisions:

1. **Ask yourself:** Is this a need or a want? If it's a need, go ahead and budget for it. If it's a want, think about the long-term benefits. Will this purchase bring lasting happiness or just a momentary thrill? For instance, that new video game might be fun now, but will it matter in a month? On the

other hand, investing in a good pair of shoes can benefit you for years.

2. **Consider peer pressure and advertising:** These can mess with your spending decisions. Ever feel like you need the latest fashion trend because all your friends have it? Or maybe an ad made you think your life won't be complete without the newest tech. Peer influence and advertising are powerful, but remember—just because everyone else is buying something doesn't mean you have to. Stay focused on your own needs and wants, not what others are telling you.

Here's an exercise to practice:

1. Create a list of your personal needs and wants.
2. Write down everything you spend money on and categorize each item. This helps you see where your money is going and identify areas to cut back.
3. Track a week's worth of spending on wants, then imagine putting that money into savings instead. How much would you have at the end of the month? Seeing the potential savings can be a real eye-opener.

Distinguishing between needs and wants is a crucial skill for managing your money effectively. By using this decision-making process, you can make smarter choices and avoid the pitfalls of impulse spending. Understand that peer pressure and advertising are designed to influence your decisions, but you have the power to stay in control. Practicing these skills now will set you up for financial success in the future.

So, the next time you're tempted to splurge, pause and think it over. Your wallet—and your future self—will thank you.

REMEMBER: Understanding the basics of financial literacy is key to navigating the complexities of managing money. Whether it's differentiating between needs and wants or setting financial goals, these foundational skills will serve you well throughout your life. Take the time to learn, practice, and apply these principles. By doing so, you'll achieve financial stability and gain the confidence to make informed decisions that align with your life goals.

CHAPTER 2
BUDGETING SKILLS FOR SUCCESS

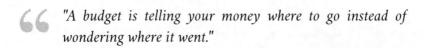 *"A budget is telling your money where to go instead of wondering where it went."*

DAVE RAMSEY

Picture this: You just got your first paycheck from that part-time job at the local café. You're feeling on top of the world. But by the end of the week, your wallet is empty, and you're left with a sense of regret over those impulse buys. Sound familiar? Don't worry, you're not alone. This chapter is all about turning that paycheck into a well-oiled financial machine. We're going to dive into the world of budgeting—and I promise it's not as boring as it sounds. In fact, it can be pretty empowering.

2.1 CREATING YOUR FIRST BUDGET: A STEP-BY-STEP GUIDE

Let's start with the basics: What exactly is a budget? Think of a budget as your financial game plan. It's a way to tell your money where to go, instead of wondering where it went. A budget helps you manage your money by tracking what you earn and what you spend. It's like having a roadmap for your finances, guiding you toward your goals without veering off course.

So, why is budgeting crucial—especially for teens? First, it helps you develop good money management habits that will serve you well throughout your life. Second, it gives you control over your money. Instead of feeling like your paycheck disappears into a black hole, you'll know exactly where it's going. Finally, a budget allows you to save for the things that matter most to you.

Ready to create your first budget? Here's a step-by-step guide to get you started, and the workbook included will help reinforce these concepts.

Step 1: List Your Sources of Income

First, list all your sources of income. This could be your allowance, earnings from a part-time job, or even money you get for doing chores around the house. Write down each source and the amount you receive from it.

Step 2: Categorize Your Expenses

Next, categorize your expenses. Expenses fall into two main categories: **fixed** and **variable**. Fixed expenses are things you pay for regularly and don't change much, like your phone bill or savings contributions. Variable expenses, on the other hand, are things that can fluctuate, like money spent on snacks, entertainment, or clothes. Breaking down your expenses into these categories will give you a clear picture of where your money is going.

Step 3: Allocate Money to Each Category

Now, this is where the magic happens. Take your total income and divide it among your expenses. Start with the essentials—your fixed expenses—then move on to your variable expenses. Make sure you also allocate money for savings. Even if it's just a small amount, setting something aside each month can make a big difference over time.

The goal is to ensure that your expenses don't exceed your income. If they do, you'll need to adjust your spending to stay within your budget.

Here's a sample budget to help you visualize how to allocate your money:

Sample Monthly Budget for a Teen

Income:

- Part-time job: $200
- Allowance: $50
- Total Income: $250

Fixed Expenses:

1. Phone bill: $30
2. Savings (Pay yourself first!): $25 (10% of income)
3. Subscription (Music/Streaming): $10
4. Total Fixed Expenses: $65

Variable Expenses:

1. Snacks/Food: $40
2. Clothing: $30
3. Entertainment (Movies, hanging out with friends): $50
4. Miscellaneous (Games, school supplies, etc.): $20
5. Total Variable Expenses: $140

Total Expenses (Fixed + Variable): $205
Remaining Balance: $250 - $205 = $45

What To Do with the Extra Money:

- You could add more to your **savings** or put some into a **long-term savings goal** (like saving up for a new phone, concert tickets, or college).
- Maybe allocate a bit to a **fun fund** for spontaneous purchases.

This sample budget shows how to manage income, cover essentials, and still have room for some fun and saving for future goals. It also reinforces the importance of putting some money aside in savings, no matter how small.

Personal monthly budget

Projected monthly income

Income 1	$4,300.00
Extra income	$300.00
Total monthly income	**$4,600.00**

Actual monthly income

Income 1	$4,000.00
Extra income	$300.00
Total monthly income	**$4,300.00**

Projected balance (Projected income minus expenses)	$3,405.00
Actual balance (Actual income minus expenses)	$3,064.00
Difference (Actual minus projected)	($341.00)

Housing

Category	Projected cost	Actual cost	Difference
Mortgage or rent	$1,000.00	$1,000.00	$0.00
Phone	$30.00	$200.00	-$46.00
Electricity	$44.00	$56.00	-$12.00
Gas	$22.00	$28.00	-$6.00
Water and sewer	$8.00	$8.00	$0.00
Cable	$34.00	$34.00	$0.00
Waste removal	$10.00	$10.00	$0.00
Maintenance or repairs	$23.00	$0.00	$23.00
Supplies	$0.00	$0.00	$0.00
Other	$0.00	$0.00	$0.00
Subtotal			**-$41.00**

Entertainment

Category	Projected cost	Actual cost	Difference
Video/DVD			$0.00
CDs			$0.00
Movies			$0.00
Concerts			$0.00
Sporting events			$0.00
Live theater			$0.00
Other			$0.00
Other			$0.00
Other			$0.00
Subtotal			**$0.00**

Transportation

Category	Projected cost	Actual cost	Difference
Vehicle payment			$0.00
Bus/taxi fare			$0.00
Insurance			$0.00
Licensing			$0.00
Fuel			$0.00
Maintenance			$0.00
Other			$0.00
Subtotal			**$0.00**

Loans

Category	Projected cost	Actual cost	Difference
Personal			$0.00
Student			$0.00
Credit card			$0.00
Credit card			$0.00
Credit card			$0.00
Other			$0.00
Subtotal			**$0.00**

Insurance

Category	Projected cost	Actual cost	Difference
Home			$0.00

Taxes

Category	Projected cost	Actual cost	Difference
Federal			$0.00

Now, let's look at a sample budget closer to your likely situation. Suppose you have a monthly income of $200. Your fixed expenses might include a $20 phone bill and $30 for savings, leaving you with $150 for variable expenses. You might allocate $50 for school supplies, $50 for entertainment, and $50 for miscellaneous expenses. And just like that, you've created your budget!

Maintaining your budget is just as important as creating it. Regularly review and adjust your budget to keep it relevant. Life happens, and your expenses might change from month to month. Set reminders to review your budget at least once a month. Look at your spending, see where adjustments are needed, and tweak your allocations as necessary. This will help you stay on track and avoid any financial surprises. You'll hear a lot more about budgeting throughout the book.

2.2 TRACKING YOUR SPENDING: TOOLS AND TECHNIQUES

Imagine you've just received your allowance or paycheck from a part-time job. You feel rich for a moment, but a week later, you're scraping together change for a soda. What happened? This might be due to something called the **Diderot Effect**, named after the creator of the encyclopedia. He bought one unnecessary expensive item, which led to a spiral of additional spending until he was broke. The lesson here is about **untracked spending**.

Knowing where your money goes is crucial for several reasons. First, it prevents overspending. When you don't track your spending, it's easy to burn through cash without realizing it. Second, tracking your expenses helps you identify patterns. Maybe you're spending more on snacks than you thought, or those small daily purchases are adding up to a big chunk of your budget.

Luckily, there are plenty of tools to help you track your spending. You don't need to be a financial wizard to get started. **Budgeting Apps** like **Mint** and **You Need a Budget** (YNAB) are excellent choices. These apps link to your bank accounts and credit cards, automatically categorizing your expenses so you can see where your money is going at a glance. Mint is great for beginners, offering a user-friendly interface and helpful alerts. YNAB focuses more on goal setting and offers educational resources to help you build better financial habits.

If you prefer a more hands-on approach, manual tracking methods like **expense diaries** are effective too. Grab a notebook or use a simple spreadsheet to jot down every expense. This method may seem old-school, but it's incredibly useful in raising awareness of your spending habits. Plus, writing things down can make the experience more tangible and provide a clearer picture of your finances.

To maximize the benefits of these tools, it's essential to use them effectively. Start by setting up categories in your chosen app or diary—such as food, entertainment, transportation, and savings. Be specific enough to understand where your money is going, but not so detailed that it feels overwhelming. Then, make it a habit to record your expenses daily. Many apps offer notifications and alerts, reminding you to log your expenses or warning you when you're nearing your budget limits. Use these features to stay on track.

Take Julia, for example. A high school student, she found herself constantly running out of money. After using Mint to track her spending, she discovered she was spending $50 a month on snacks at the school cafeteria. By packing her lunch a few days a week, she saved money and redirected it toward her savings goal of buying a new laptop. Another example is Jake, who kept an expense diary. He realized he was spending too much on weekend outings with friends. By setting a limit on his entertainment budget and sticking to it, he managed to save more and even had money left over for unexpected expenses.

Tracking your spending might seem tedious at first, but it's a powerful tool for taking control of your finances. Whether you use an app or a notebook, the important thing is to be consistent. You'll be amazed at how much you learn about your spending habits and how easy it becomes to make adjustments.

2.3 ADJUSTING YOUR BUDGET: STAYING FLEXIBLE

Let's face it, life is unpredictable. One minute you're cruising along, and the next, you're hit with an unexpected expense that throws your budget into chaos. That's why it's crucial to keep your budget flexible. Imagine you've been saving diligently for a new phone, but suddenly, you need to buy supplies for a surprise school project. Or perhaps your part-time job hours get cut, reducing your income. These changes can wreak havoc on a rigid budget. Flexibility allows you to adapt to these curveballs without derailing your financial goals.

Unplanned expenses are a reality of life, and this is why budgeting and savings are important. A flexible budget helps you manage these surprises without feeling overwhelmed. Similarly, changes in income can affect your financial planning. Maybe your hours get cut at work, or you receive a bonus for excellent performance. Being able to adjust your budget to reflect these changes ensures that you're always living within your means and making the most of your resources.

So, how do you adjust your budget when life throws you a curve-ball? Start by reallocating funds between categories. If you've budgeted $50 for entertainment but need $20 for that unexpected school project, shift some of your entertainment money to cover the new expense. It's all about balance. Next, look for ways to cut back on non-essential expenses. Maybe skip that extra latte or hold off on buying new clothes for a month. By trimming unnecessary spending, you can free up funds for urgent needs. Increasing your savings contributions is another smart move. If you find yourself with extra income, like a birthday gift or a bonus, consider putting a portion into savings. This way, you're building a cushion for future unexpected expenses.

Regular budget reviews are crucial for maintaining flexibility. Set aside time each month to review your budget and see how well it's working. Are there categories where you consistently overspend? Are there areas where you could cut back? Monthly check-ins help you catch issues early and make adjustments before they become big problems. Seasonal adjustments are important too. Your spending might change depending on the time of year—like spending more on entertainment during the summer when you're out of school, or having extra expenses during the holiday season. Adjusting your budget to reflect these seasonal changes ensures you're always prepared.

Staying flexible with your budget is all about being proactive and adaptable. Life is full of surprises, and your budget should be able to roll with the punches. By reallocating funds, cutting back on non-essential expenses, and regularly reviewing your budget, you can stay on track and achieve your financial goals without unnecessary stress. Remember, a budget is a tool to help you manage your money, not a rigid set of rules to follow blindly. Keep it flexible, and you'll be better equipped to handle whatever life throws your way.

2.4 BUDGETING FOR FUN: ALLOWING ROOM FOR ENTERTAINMENT

You've been diligently tracking your spending, sticking to your budget, and saving for your goals. But what's the point of all this financial discipline if you're not having any fun? Including entertainment in your budget is crucial for maintaining balance. You need to reward yourself for your hard work and avoid the burnout that can come from being too strict with your money. Think of it as treating yourself without feeling guilty. Life is meant to be enjoyed, and budgeting for fun ensures you can do that without wrecking your financial plans.

So, how do you allocate money for fun without going overboard? Start by setting a monthly entertainment budget. Decide on an amount you're comfortable spending on leisure activities each month. This gives you a clear limit, so you can enjoy yourself without the stress of overspending.

Next, prioritize your activities. What do you enjoy most? Whether it's going to the movies, hanging out with friends, or indulging in a hobby, focus your entertainment budget on activities that bring you the most joy and satisfaction. This way, you'll get the most bang for your buck.

There are plenty of budget-friendly entertainment options that won't break the bank. For instance, movie nights at home can be just as fun as going to the theater. Grab some popcorn, find a movie on a streaming service, and invite a few friends over. If you enjoy the outdoors, activities like hiking or biking are great—and the best part is, they're free!

Finding deals and discounts is another smart way to save on entertainment. Always be on the lookout for student discounts. Many places, from movie theaters to restaurants, offer special rates for students—so don't forget your student ID. Free local events are also a great option. Check out community boards, social media, or local websites for events like concerts, outdoor festivals, or art exhibits. These events allow you to have fun without spending a dime.

Planning ahead can also help save money. Booking tickets or making reservations in advance often comes with discounts. For example, many theaters offer lower prices for advance bookings or weekday showings. Planning group activities is another way to save. Splitting the cost of outings with friends—like carpooling to a concert or sharing expenses for a road trip—can make your entertainment budget stretch further.

Budgeting for fun isn't just about spending money; it's about spending it wisely and making sure you enjoy life while staying financially responsible. You can have the best of both worlds by setting a budget, prioritizing your favorite activities, and finding ways to save. So go ahead—plan that movie night, take that hike, or start that DIY project. You've earned it!

2.5 BUDGETING CHALLENGES: OVERCOMING COMMON HURDLES

Budgeting can sound easy in theory, but real life often throws a few curveballs. One of the most common challenges teens face is **impulse spending.** Picture this: You Walk into a store just to browse, and before you know it, you're walking out with a new pair of sneakers you didn't plan on buying. Impulse spending can quickly derail even the best budget. The key to overcoming this challenge is to create a **buffer for unexpected expenses.** Set aside a small amount each month specifically for impulse buys. This way, you can indulge occasionally without wrecking your budget. Think of it as a safety net for those spontaneous moments.

Another big hurdle is **peer pressure.** Maybe your friends are going to the latest concert, and you feel pressure to join them, even if it means spending money you don't have. Setting boundaries with friends is crucial. Be upfront about your financial goals and let them know you're on a budget. True friends will understand and respect your decisions. Suggest alternative activities that are more budget-friendly—you might be surprised how many of your friends are also looking for ways to save and would appreciate the suggestion.

Irregular income can also complicate budgeting. If you have a part-time job with fluctuating hours, your paycheck might look different each month. This makes it hard to plan and stick to a consistent budget. One effective strategy is using **savings** to manage irregular income. When you get a larger paycheck, put a portion into savings. This helps smooth out fluctuations and ensures you have enough to cover expenses during leaner months. Treat your savings like a financial buffer that helps you handle the ups and downs of inconsistent income.

Take the story of Samantha, a high school student who struggled with peer pressure. Her friends often went out to eat, but she wanted to save money for a summer trip. Instead of giving in, she suggested having potluck dinners at home, where each friend brought a dish. Not only did this save money, but it also became a fun tradition everyone looked forward to. Another example is Alex, who had a part-time job with unpredictable hours. He overcame the challenge by saving a portion of his higher paychecks in a separate account and was able to maintain a financial buffer when his hours were cut.

These examples show that with a bit of creativity and planning, you can overcome common budgeting challenges.

Staying motivated can also be tough, especially when it feels like you're constantly making sacrifices. One way to stay motivated is by **celebrating small financial victories**. Did you stick to your budget this month? Treat yourself to a little reward. These small celebrations can keep you motivated and make budgeting feel less like a chore. Keeping your long-term goals in mind is also crucial. Whenever you're tempted to splurge, remind yourself why you're budgeting in the first place. Whether it's saving for college, a trip, or a major purchase, keeping your eyes on the prize will help you stay focused.

Finally, remember that **budgeting is a skill** that takes time to master. You might stumble along the way, and that's okay. The important thing is to learn from your mistakes and keep going. Think of each budgeting challenge as a learning opportunity that brings you one step closer to financial independence. With patience and persistence, you can overcome any hurdle and achieve your financial goals.

REMEMBER:

Budgeting can feel overwhelming, but it's all about taking it one step at a time. By addressing common challenges like impulse spending, peer pressure, and irregular income, you can stay on track and make your money work for you. Keep celebrating your small wins, and always remind yourself of the bigger picture. Up next, we'll dive into the world of saving money the smart way.

CHAPTER 3
SAVING MONEY THE
SMART WAY

"Do not save what is left after spending; instead, spend what is left after saving."

WARREN BUFFETT

Ever wonder how some people always seem to have extra cash for the latest tech, spontaneous road trips, or even emergencies, while others are perpetually broke? Warren Buffet's quote says it all. The secret isn't necessarily landing a high-paying job or winning the lottery—it's mastering the art of saving. Yep, you heard that right. Saving money is a superpower that can transform your financial future. Imagine having a stash of cash that you can tap into whenever you need it. Sounds pretty sweet, right? Let's dive into why saving money is so crucial and how you can get started today.

3.1 THE POWER OF SAVING: WHY IT'S ESSENTIAL

Saving money is like planting a seed that grows into a mighty tree, providing shade and fruit for years to come. It's not just about having extra cash to splurge on your favorite things—although that's definitely a perk. The real magic of saving lies in the financial security and opportunities it brings. First off, savings give you financial independence. You won't have to rely on your parents or scramble for a loan when an unexpected expense pops up. Whether it's a sudden car repair or a surprise medical bill, having savings means you're prepared. No more panic attacks or borrowing money at sky-high interest rates (Remember our mindset discussion? Reduce the stress!).

But that's not all. Saving money opens up a world of opportunities for investment. Imagine you stumble upon a fantastic business idea or a lucrative investment opportunity down the road. Having savings allows you to seize these chances without hesitation. It's like having a golden ticket that lets you take advantage of opportunities that come your way. Plus, the more you save, the more you can invest, and the more your money can grow. It's a win-win situation.

From the previous chapters, you know the earlier you start, the more time your money has to grow. This is where the magic of compound interest comes into play. Compound interest is like a snowball rolling down a hill, gathering more snow and growing bigger as it goes. When you save money, you earn interest on your initial amount. Over time, you also earn interest on the interest you've already earned. It's like your money is working for you, earning more money even while you sleep.

Let's break it down with a simple example. Imagine you save $10 a week. After one year, you'd have $520. But here's where it gets exciting. If you put that $520 into a savings account with a compound interest rate of 5%, by the end of five years, you'd have around $670. That's an extra $150 just from letting your money sit and grow.

The difference between simple and compound interest is significant. Simple interest only earns you money on your initial deposit, while compound interest earns you money on both your initial deposit and the interest you've already accumulated. Over time, this can make a huge difference in your savings.

The power of saving and compound interest becomes even more evident when you hear real-life stories of teens who have successfully saved money. Sarah, for example, started saving a portion of her allowance and part-time job earnings from a young age. By the time she graduated high school, she had saved enough to cover a significant portion of her college tuition. This not only reduced her reliance on student loans but also set her up for financial success in the future. Then there's Jake, a young entrepreneur who used his savings to start a small online business. By saving diligently and reinvesting his profits, he was able to grow his business and achieve financial independence—before turning twenty!

These stories show that saving money isn't just a theoretical concept—it's a powerful tool that can change your life. Whether your goal is to pay for college, start a business, or simply have a financial cushion for peace of mind, saving money is the key. It's about developing good habits, starting early, and letting the power of compound interest work its magic. So, grab a piggy bank, open a savings account, or use a savings app, and start saving today. Your future self will thank you!

3.2 BUILDING AN EMERGENCY FUND: YOUR SAFETY NET

Imagine this: you're on your way to school, and out of nowhere, your bike tire goes flat. Or maybe you're a little older and you're hit with an unexpected medical bill after a surprise visit to the doctor. These are the kinds of moments when an emergency fund can be a lifesaver. An emergency fund is simply a stash of money set aside to cover unexpected expenses. Think of it as your financial safety net, catching you when life throws you a curveball. Whether it's a sudden car repair or an urgent trip to visit a sick relative, having an emergency fund means you won't have to scramble for cash or, worse, go into debt.

Starting an emergency fund is easier than you think. The first step is to set a target amount. A good rule of thumb is to aim for at least $500 to start. This might seem like a lot, but you don't have to save it all at once. Break it down into manageable chunks. If you can save $50 a month, you'll reach your goal in ten months. The key is to make saving a regular habit. Allocate a portion of your income to your emergency fund every time you get paid. Whether it's your allowance, earnings from a part-time job, or even birthday money, put a percentage aside for emergencies. Consistency is key.

Now that you've decided to build an emergency fund, where do you keep it? You want your emergency fund to be easily accessible but not so easy that you're tempted to dip into it for non-emergencies. High-yield savings accounts are a good option. They offer higher interest rates than regular savings accounts, so your money grows faster. Plus, these accounts are usually easy to access in case of an emergency. Another smart move is to keep your emergency fund in a separate bank account. This way, you're less likely to spend it on impulse buys. It's out of sight but still within reach when you need it.

But what exactly qualifies as an emergency? Let's look at some scenarios. Imagine you wake up with a toothache that just won't quit. A trip to the dentist reveals you need a filling, and it's not cheap. This is a perfect example of when to use your emergency fund. Another scenario could be a sudden travel need. Maybe a close family member falls ill, and you need to book a last-minute flight to be with them. Your emergency fund can cover the cost without causing financial strain. The idea is to use this money for true emergencies, not for that new game or a night out with friends.

REMEMBER:

Building an emergency fund is all about preparation and peace of mind. It's not about expecting the worst but being ready if it happens. Start small, be consistent, and keep your fund in a safe, accessible place. You'll be amazed at how empowering it feels to know you have a financial safety net ready to catch you when life's little surprises come your way.

CHAPTER 4
EARNING MONEY AS A TEEN

 "The secret to getting ahead is getting started."

MARK TWAIN

Picture this: you're at the mall with your friends, and you spot the coolest Pumas ever. You check your wallet, and bam, you're broke. Sound familiar? Earning your own money not only gets you those awesome sneaks, but also teaches you valuable life skills. Whether you want to save for college, help out at home, or just have some extra cash for fun, finding ways to earn money as a teen is a game-changer. This chapter is all about exploring different ways to make money, starting with the classic part-time job.

4.1 PART-TIME JOBS: FINDING AND BALANCING WORK

Part-time jobs can be a great way to earn money, but where do you start? Finding a part-time job suitable for teens is simpler than you might think. First, consider local businesses and retail stores. These places often have flexible hours and are used to hiring teens. Think about your favorite hangout spots—cafes, fast-food joints, clothing stores, or even the local video game shop. Walk in, ask if they're hiring, and be prepared to fill out an application on the spot. Showing initiative can make a great first impression.

Another great resource is online job portals specifically designed for teens. Websites like Snagajob, Indeed, and local community job boards can be goldmines for finding part-time work. These platforms allow you to filter jobs based on location, hours, and type of work, making it easy to find something that fits into your schedule. Don't forget to check out job postings at your school's career center or bulletin boards. Schools often have connections with local businesses looking to hire students.

Networking is another powerful tool. Talk to family and friends about your job hunt. They might know someone who's hiring or can recommend you for a position. Sometimes, the best opportunities come from word of mouth. For example, your neighbor might need help with yard work or babysitting, or a family friend might own a business looking for part-time help. Don't underestimate the power of your personal network.

Balancing work and school is crucial. You don't want your grades to suffer because you're working too many hours. Start by creating a weekly schedule. Map out your school hours, homework time, extracurricular activities, and social commitments. Then, see where you can fit in work hours without overwhelming yourself. Prioritize your tasks and set limits. It's okay to say no to extra shifts if it means keeping your workload manageable. Avoiding burnout is key—make sure you're leaving enough time for rest and relaxation. Remember, school and your well-being come first.

Excelling in a part-time job isn't just about showing up; it's about making the most of the opportunity. Developing a strong work ethic is essential. Be punctual, dependable, and willing to go the extra mile. Show your employer that you're serious about your job. Communicating effectively with your supervisors is also important. If you're unsure about a task or need help, don't hesitate to ask questions. Clear communication can prevent misunderstandings and show that you're proactive.

Seeking feedback for improvement is another way to stand out. Regularly ask your supervisor how you're doing and if there are areas where you can improve. This not only helps you grow but also shows that you're committed to doing your best. For instance, if you're working at a local cafe, ask your manager for tips on improving your customer service skills or making drinks more efficiently. Small improvements can make a big difference.

Examples:

- **Mia**, a high school student, worked at a local cafe. She started as a cashier but quickly learned how to make drinks and handle customer service. By asking for extra shifts during the weekends and holidays, she earned enough to buy her first laptop. Her manager even wrote her a glowing recommendation letter for college.
- **Tom**, another high school student, worked at a bookstore. He balanced his job with school by creating a detailed schedule and sticking to it. With his earnings, he saved for a summer trip abroad, an experience that enriched his life and made his college application stand out.

Earning money through a part-time job teaches you responsibility, time management, and the value of hard work. Whether you're working at a local cafe or retail store, the skills and experiences you gain will benefit you in the long run. So, start applying, and watch as your hard-earned money opens up new opportunities and helps you achieve your goals.

4.2 SIDE HUSTLES: CREATIVE WAYS TO EARN EXTRA CASH

When you think about earning extra cash, a part-time job isn't the only option. Side hustles can be a fantastic way to make money while giving you the flexibility to explore your interests and passions. Unlike traditional jobs, side hustles allow you to work on your own terms and schedule. Want to fit in some work between school and soccer practice? No problem. Side hustles offer that kind of flexibility.

Let's dive into some creative side hustle ideas you can start right away:

- **Pet sitting or dog walking** is a great option if you love animals. Many people need someone to look after their pets while they're at work or on vacation.
- **Babysitting for neighbors** is another classic side hustle that never goes out of style. If you're good with kids, this can be both fun and rewarding.
- **Lawn mowing and yard work** are perfect if you don't mind getting your hands dirty. Many homeowners are willing to pay for help with their gardens and lawns.
- **Tutoring younger students** is a fantastic way to earn money while helping others. If you excel in a particular subject, offering tutoring services can be a great way to share your knowledge and make some cash.

Once you've decided on a side hustle, the next step is marketing it. **Creating flyers** is an old-school but effective way to get the word out. Design a simple, eye-catching flyer with your services, rates, and contact information. Post them around your neighborhood, local community centers, and even your school. **Social media** can also be a powerful tool. Share your side hustle on your social media profiles, join local community groups, and encourage your friends and family to share your posts. **Word-of-mouth recommendations** can be incredibly effective. Tell your neighbors, friends, and family about your side hustle and ask them to spread the word.

Examples:

- **Trent** started a pet-sitting business at 15. He created flyers, posted them around his neighborhood, and shared his services on social media. Within a few months, he had a steady stream of clients. He loved animals and used the money he earned to save for a summer camp he had always wanted to attend.
- **Emma**, a high school student, excelled in math and started tutoring younger students. She began by helping her younger brother's friends, and soon word spread. Within a year, she had multiple clients and was earning enough to save for her college fund.

Side hustles not only provide extra cash but also teach valuable skills like time management, customer service, and marketing. They give you the chance to turn your interests into income while working on your own schedule. So, why not start a side hustle today and see where it takes you?

CHAPTER 5
BANKING BASICS

 "Why do you rob banks? Cause that's where the money is!"

WILLIE SUTTON, FAMOUS BANK ROBBER OF
THE 1950S

Picture this: You've just scored your first paycheck, and it's burning a hole in your pocket. You're torn between saving for that new game console and splurging on a weekend outing with friends. Here's where banking comes in handy. Opening a bank account is like giving your money a cozy, secure home where it can grow and stay safe until you need it. Plus, it's the first step toward managing your finances like a pro. But before you dive into the world of banking, let's break down the basics.

5.1 OPENING YOUR FIRST BANK ACCOUNT: WHAT YOU NEED TO KNOW

First things first, let's talk about the different types of bank accounts you can open. Imagine bank accounts as different rooms in a house, each serving a unique purpose. A **checking account** is like your living room—a space for daily activities. It's designed for everyday transactions like paying for groceries, streaming subscriptions, or that daily iced coffee. With a checking account, you can write checks, use a debit card, and make online payments. It's your go-to account for spending money.

On the flip side, a **savings account** is more like your attic—a place to store things for the future. This account is perfect for stashing away money you don't plan to spend right away. Whether you're saving for college, a new laptop, or an emergency fund, a savings account keeps your money safe while earning a bit of interest. Think of it as your financial cushion—there when you need it, but not as easily accessible as your checking account.

Then there are **joint accounts**, which are like shared spaces in a house where everyone has access. These accounts are great for teens and parents who want to manage money together. A joint account allows both you and your parents to deposit and with-draw money, making it easier to monitor spending and savings. It's a fantastic way to learn financial responsibility with a bit of parental oversight.

Ready to open your first bank account? Here's a step-by-step guide to make the process as smooth as possible. First, choose the right bank and account type. Consider what you need the account for—daily transactions, saving money, or both. Research different banks to find one that offers the best features for your needs. For instance, some banks have no monthly fees, while others offer higher interest rates on savings accounts. Once you've decided, gather the required documents. You'll need a government-issued ID (like a driver's license or passport), proof of address (like a utility bill or school document), and your Social Security number.

Next, head to the bank or hop online to complete the application process. If you're applying in person, visit a local branch and fill out the necessary forms. If you're going the online route, most banks have easy-to-follow application forms on their websites. You'll need to provide your personal information, upload your documents, and sometimes make an initial deposit. Double-check all your information before submitting the application to avoid any delays.

Before finalizing your choice, research **bank fees and services**. Not all bank accounts are created equal, and some come with hidden costs. For example, some banks charge monthly mainte-nance fees just to keep the account open. Others have minimum balance requirements, meaning you'll need to keep a certain amount of money in the account to avoid fees. ATM and transac-tion fees are also something to watch out for. If you use an out-of-network ATM, you might get hit with extra charges. Knowing these fees upfront can help you avoid unpleasant surprises.

When choosing a bank, consider its **reputation and customer service**. A bank with a good reputation is likely to offer better service and more reliable products. Look for reviews online or ask friends and family for recommendations. The convenience of branch and ATM locations is another important factor. You don't want to drive miles just to withdraw cash or deposit a check. Check if the bank has locations and ATMs near your home, school, or workplace.

Finally, make sure the bank offers robust **online and mobile banking** features. In today's digital age, managing your money from your phone or computer makes life much easier. Look for features like mobile check deposit, real-time transaction alerts, and easy access to account information. A good banking app can save you a trip to the branch and make managing your finances more convenient.

Opening your first bank account is a big step toward financial independence. By understanding the different types of accounts, gathering the necessary documents, and choosing the right bank, you'll set yourself up for success. So, get ready to give your money a safe and cozy home where it can grow and support your financial goals.

5.2 UNDERSTANDING BANK STATEMENTS: A SIMPLE GUIDE

Imagine getting a letter from your bank, and it looks like it's written in a secret code. That's pretty much what a bank statement can feel like if you don't know how to read it. But once you crack the code, you'll see it's a treasure trove of information about your money. A **bank statement** is essentially a detailed record of your account activity over a specific period—usually a month. Let's break down the different parts of a bank statement so you can read it like a pro.

First up is the **Account Summary**. This section gives you a snapshot of your account's health. It shows the opening balance, which is the amount of money in your account at the start of the period, and the closing balance, which is the amount at the end. It's like a quick before-and-after picture of your finances. If you see that your closing balance is consistently lower than your opening balance, it might be time to rethink your spending habits.

Next, we have the **List of Transactions**. This is where the nitty-gritty details live. Every deposit, withdrawal, and transfer you've made during the period is listed here. Deposits can include your paycheck, birthday money, or any other cash you've put into your account. Withdrawals are the money you've taken out, whether through ATM withdrawals, debit card purchases, or online payments. Transfers can be money you've moved between accounts, like from checking to savings. Each transaction will have a date, description, and amount, making it easy to track where your money is going.

Then, there are the **fees and interest earned**. This part shows any charges the bank has deducted from your account, like monthly maintenance fees or ATM fees. It also shows any interest you've earned if you have a savings account or an interest-bearing checking account. While fees can feel like a bummer, earning interest is like getting a little bonus for keeping your money in the bank.

So, how do you read and interpret a bank statement? Start by identifying and verifying each transaction. Go through the list and make sure you recognize everything. If you see a charge from a store you've never visited, it might be an unauthorized transaction. Next, check for errors. Sometimes banks make mistakes, so it's essential to review your statement carefully. Look for duplicate charges, incorrect amounts, or fees you weren't expecting. If you spot any discrepancies, contact your bank right away to get them sorted out.

Regularly reviewing your bank statements is crucial for several reasons. First, it helps you **monitor your spending habits**. By seeing where your money goes each month, you can identify patterns and adjust if needed. Maybe you're spending more on eating out than you realized, and cutting back could help you save. Second, it's a vital tool for detecting **fraud or identity theft**. If someone has accessed your account and made unauthorized transactions, reviewing your statement can help you catch it early and take action. Lastly, ensuring the **accuracy of your bank records** is essential for maintaining financial health. Errors happen, and catching them quickly can save you from potential headaches down the line.

Sample Bank Statement for Practice

Let's look at a sample bank statement to put this into practice. Imagine the following details:

In this example, you can see how the account balance changed over the month. Each transaction is dated and described, making it easy to verify and understand. The account summary gives a clear picture of your financial standing at the start and end of the period. With practice, reading your bank statement will become second nature, and you'll be able to keep a close eye on your money.

█▌CHOICE

JRMartin Choice Bank
West Virginia
P O Box 990180
Country Roads, WV 70826-0180

July 1, 2018 through July 31, 2018
Primary Account: **00000958581485**

CUSTOMER SERVICE INFORMATION

WebSite:	www.choicebank.com
Service Center:	1-800-555-9935
Hearing Impaired:	1-800-555-7383
Para Espanol:	1-877-555-4273
International Calls:	1-713-555-1679

Contact us by phone for questions, on this statement, change information, and general inquiries, 24 hours a day, 7 days a week

ldldl.dldddl dlludlddldllu.ull.ldl ldlldldlldldlddlldlulddlldllu.lldl
00013422 DBA 001 LA 1020S – YY N T 1 0000000007 0000
Company Name
Company Address
State, Zip

Account Summary

Opening Balance	$5,234.09
Withdrawals	$2,395.67
Deposits	$2,872.45
Closing Balance on Apr 18, 2010	**$9,710.87**

Your Transaction Details

Date	Details	Withdrawals	Deposits	Balance
Apr 8	Opening Balance			5,234.09
Apr 8	Insurance		272.45	5,506.54
Apr 10	ATM	200.00		5,306.54
Apr 12	Internet Transfer		250.00	5,556.54
Apr 12	Payroll		2100.00	7,656.54
Apr 13	Bill payment	135.07		7,521.47
Apr 14	Direct debit	200.00		7,321.47
Apr 14	Deposit		250.00	7,567.87
Apr 15	Bill payment	525.72		7,042.15
Apr 17	Bill payment	327.63		6,714.52
Apr 17	Bill payment	729.96		5,984.56
Apr 18	Insurance		272.45	5,506.54
Apr 18	ATM	200.00		5,306.54
Apr 18	Internet Transfer		250.00	5,556.54
Apr 18	Payroll		2100.00	7,656.54
Apr 18	Bill payment	135.07		7,521.47
Apr 19	Direct debit	200.00		7,321.47
Apr 19	Deposit		250.00	7,567.87
Apr 19	Bill payment	525.72		7,042.15
Apr 20	Bill payment	327.63		6,714.52
Apr 20	Bill payment	729.96		5,984.56
Apr 20	Deposit		250.00	7,567.87
Apr 20	Bill payment	525.72		7,042.15
Apr 20	Bill payment	327.63		6,714.52
Apr 21	Bill payment	729.96		5,984.56
	Closing Balance			**$9,710.87**

Oh, one other thing: Does the Closing Balance on this sample look right?

No! It is wrong. If the Opening Balance was $5234.09, the Withdrawals were $2395.67, and the Deposits were $2872.45, then the Closing Balance should be $5740.87.

REMEMBER:

Understanding your bank statement is a valuable skill that helps you manage your finances effectively. By knowing how to read and interpret each section, regularly reviewing your statements, and checking for errors or unauthorized transactions, you can stay on top of your financial game. So, next time that letter from the bank arrives, you'll be ready to decode it with confidence.

5.3 USING ATMS AND ONLINE BANKING SAFELY

Picture this: you need cash for a night out with friends, so you head to the nearest ATM. Seems simple enough, right? While ATMs are incredibly convenient, it's essential to use them safely. Start by choosing well-lit, secure locations. Look for ATMs inside banks or in well-trafficked areas. Avoid isolated spots, especially at night. When you're at the ATM, be aware of your surroundings. Keep an eye out for anyone lingering nearby or acting suspiciously. It's always better to be safe than sorry. When entering your PIN, cover the keypad with your hand or body. It might feel like you're acting in a spy movie, but this simple act can prevent someone from seeing your PIN and potentially accessing your account.

Online banking is another game-changer. Imagine the convenience of checking your account balance while waiting for your friend to join a group chat or transferring money between accounts without leaving your couch. Online banking platforms offer a wide range of features that make managing your finances a breeze. You can pay bills online, set up automatic payments, and even track your spending with just a few clicks. Need to transfer money to your savings account? No problem. Want to pay your phone bill without writing a check? Done. Managing your accounts from anywhere, at any time, is a massive advantage, especially for teens who are always on the go.

However, with great convenience comes the need for extra caution. Online banking requires you to be vigilant about protecting your personal information. Start by using strong, unique passwords for your accounts. Avoid easily guessed passwords like "password123" or your birthday. Instead, create passwords with a mix of letters, numbers, and symbols. Enabling two-factor authentication adds an extra layer of security. This means even if someone gets hold of your password, they'll need a second form of identification to access your account, like a code sent to your phone. It's also crucial to avoid using public Wi-Fi for banking transactions. Public networks can be less secure, making it easier for hackers to intercept your information. Stick to your home network or use a secure mobile connection.

Regularly updating your security software is another must-do. Keeping your operating system, antivirus software, and browser up to date ensures you have the latest security patches to protect against new threats. It might seem like a hassle, but these updates can prevent significant headaches down the line.

Online banking opens up a world of possibilities, and most banks now offer these features. One common task is setting up automatic bill payments. This feature ensures your bills are paid on time without you having to lift a finger. You can set it and forget it, avoiding late fees and maintaining a good credit score. Viewing your transaction history is another valuable feature. It allows you to see all your account activity at a glance, making it easier to track your spending and spot any suspicious transactions. Need to keep a record of your finances? Downloading bank statements is a breeze with online banking. You can access your statements anytime, making it easier to manage your records and prepare for things like applying for financial aid or filing taxes.

REMEMBER:

Online banking offers the convenience of checking account balances, transferring money, and paying bills with just a few clicks. By using strong, unique passwords, enabling two-factor authentication, avoiding public Wi-Fi, and regularly updating security software, you can safeguard your personal information while enjoying the benefits of online banking.

5.4 MOBILE BANKING: MANAGING FINANCES ON THE GO

You now have your bank right in your pocket! That's the magic of mobile banking. With a mobile banking app, you can manage your finances from anywhere. Mobile banking offers real-time transaction alerts, so you know exactly when money goes in or out of your account. No more waiting for monthly statements to see if your paycheck has cleared or if that online purchase has gone through. Plus, you get easy access to your account information anytime you need it. Checking your balance, reviewing your spending, and transferring money between accounts can all be done with just a few taps on your phone.

Mobile banking apps come packed with features that make managing your money a breeze. One of the most convenient is **mobile check deposit**. No more trips to the bank or ATM—just snap a photo of your check with your phone's camera, and the app takes care of the rest. It's fast, easy, and incredibly convenient. **Budgeting tools and expense tracking** are another great feature.

These tools help you keep tabs on your spending, set savings goals, and see where your money is going. It's like having a personal financial advisor in your pocket. **Peer-to-peer payment options**, such as Zelle and Venmo, make it simple to split bills with friends, pay for shared expenses, or even send a gift. These services transfer money quickly and securely, ensuring you can handle your financial obligations without any hassle.

Getting started with a mobile banking app is straightforward. First, download the app from your bank's website or the app store on your phone. Once installed, open the app, and follow the prompts to link your bank accounts. You'll need your account number and possibly some additional identifying information. After linking your accounts, take a few minutes to customize your alert settings. Decide what types of notifications you want to receive, such as deposit alerts, low balance warnings, or payment reminders. This personalization helps you stay on top of your finances without being overwhelmed by constant notifications.

Security is a top priority when it comes to mobile banking. Protecting your personal data is crucial. Start by using **biometric authentication**, like fingerprint or facial recognition, to secure your app. This adds an extra layer of protection, making it harder for anyone else to access your account. Locking your phone with a passcode, pattern, or biometric lock is another essential step. This ensures that even if your phone falls into the wrong hands, your banking information remains secure. Regularly review the app permissions on your phone to ensure it only has access to the necessary information. Keeping these permissions in check can prevent unauthorized access and potential data breaches.

Mobile banking apps offer a level of convenience that traditional banking just can't match. Imagine setting up automatic bill payments while waiting for your friends to join you at the mall. Or viewing your transaction history while sipping on your favorite latte at your local café. These apps make it easy to stay on top of your finances, no matter where you are. Need to download a bank statement for your records? Done. Want to transfer money to your savings account while standing in line at the grocery store? Easy. The ability to manage your money on the go is great, especially for teens who are always on the move.

5.5 THE ROLE OF BANKS: HOW THEY HELP YOU MANAGE MONEY

Ever wonder what happens to your money when you deposit it into a bank? Think of banks as the financial superheroes of your life, working behind the scenes to keep your money safe, accessible, and growing. One of the primary functions of banks is **safeguarding deposits**. When you drop your money into a bank account, it doesn't just sit in a vault gathering dust. Instead, banks use advanced security measures to protect your funds from theft and loss. Your money is insured up to a certain amount, meaning even if the bank faces issues, your funds are safe. This security lets you sleep easy, knowing your money isn't going anywhere without your say-so.

But banks do more than just guard your cash. They also provide **loans and credit**, acting as a bridge to help you achieve your financial goals. Need a loan to buy a car, pay for college, or start a small business? Banks assess your creditworthiness and offer loans that you can pay back over time with interest. These loans make big purchases possible, even if you don't have all the money upfront. Additionally, banks offer **credit cards**, which are like short-term loans you can use for everyday purchases. If you use them wisely and pay off your balance each month, credit cards can help you build a strong credit history. More on this later.

Banks also **facilitate financial transactions**, making it easier to manage your day-to-day finances. From direct deposits to automatic bill payments, banks streamline the process of moving money around. Imagine getting your paycheck directly deposited into your account without visiting the bank. Or setting up automatic payments for your utility bills so you never miss a due date. These services save you time and hassle, letting you focus on more important things.

The benefits of banking services extend beyond just convenience. One of the biggest advantages is **earning interest on your savings**. When you deposit money into a savings account, the bank pays you interest. It's like getting a little reward for letting your money sit there. Over time, this interest can add up, helping your savings grow faster than if you kept your cash under your mattress. Access to **credit and loans** opens doors to opportunities that might otherwise be out of reach.

Banks and other financial firms also offer **financial planning and advisory services**. Need help figuring out how to save for college or plan for retirement? Many banks have financial advisors who can guide you through the process. They can help you set realistic financial goals, create a budget, and develop a plan to achieve your dreams. These services provide valuable insights and support, ensuring you make informed decisions about your money.

Beyond the basics, banks offer a variety of **additional services** that can make managing your finances easier. Safe deposit boxes provide a secure place to store valuable items like important documents, jewelry, or family heirlooms. **Investment and retirement accounts** help you plan for the future by offering ways to invest your money and grow your wealth over time. Whether it's a traditional IRA, Roth IRA, or a brokerage account, these options let you take control of your financial destiny. Banks also offer **insurance**

products, like life and disability insurance, to protect you and your loved ones from financial hardships.

REMEMBER:

Banks play a crucial role in helping you manage your money and achieve your financial goals. From safeguarding deposits and providing loans to offering financial planning and additional services, banks are here to support you every step of the way.

So, whether you're saving for college, planning to buy a home, or simply looking to grow your wealth, banks have the tools and expertise to help you succeed in your financial journey.

CHAPTER 6
SMART SPENDING AND CONSUMERISM

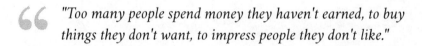 *"Too many people spend money they haven't earned, to buy things they don't want, to impress people they don't like."*

WILL ROGERS

I've referenced this type of scenario previously: You walk into a store with a crisp $20 bill, feeling like you're on top of the world. But an hour later, you're walking out with a few trinkets you didn't really need, and nothing left in your wallet. Sound familiar? It's time to change that.

Welcome to the world of smart spending and consumerism, where you'll learn how to make every dollar work for you, not against you. We'll dive into the art of frugality, smart shopping tips, and how to avoid those sneaky impulse buys. Ready to become a savvy spender? Let's go!

6.1 THE ART OF FRUGALITY: GETTING THE MOST FOR YOUR MONEY

So, what's frugality all about? Think of it as the superhero of smart spending. Frugality means being intentional with your money, making sure every dollar counts. It's not about being cheap or depriving yourself of fun; it's about prioritizing value over cost and avoiding waste. When you're frugal, you save more money, which means you can reach your financial goals faster. Plus, you'll reduce waste by only buying what you need and making the most of what you have. It's like giving your wallet a workout, making it stronger and more resilient.

One of the easiest ways to practice frugality is by comparing prices before you buy. Whether you're shopping for clothes, tech, or even groceries, take a few minutes to check different stores or websites. You'd be surprised how much you can save by simply looking around. Another fantastic frugal habit is using coupons and discounts. Many stores offer student discounts, and there are plenty of websites and apps dedicated to finding the best deals. Keep an eye out for sales, and don't be afraid to ask if there are any ongoing promotions.

Opting for second-hand items is another great way to be frugal. Thrift stores, garage sales, and online marketplaces like eBay or Facebook Marketplace are goldmines for affordable, high-quality items. You can find everything from clothes to electronics at a fraction of the cost. Plus, buying second-hand is environmentally friendly. It's a win-win! Just remember to inspect items for quality and ensure they're in good working condition before you buy.

Now, and this is important, let's clear up a common misconception: being frugal is not the same as being cheap. Frugality is about making smart choices and getting the best value for your money, while being cheap often means sacrificing quality for the lowest price. When you're frugal, you prioritize quality over quantity. You might spend a bit more on a durable pair of shoes that will last for years instead of buying several pairs of cheap ones that wear out quickly. Investing in durable goods saves you money in the long run and reduces waste.

Seeking value rather than the lowest price is a key principle of frugality. It's about finding a balance between cost and quality. For example, buying a used laptop from a reputable seller might cost more upfront than a new, low-budget model, but the used laptop will likely perform better and last longer. Frugality means thinking long-term and making choices that provide the most value over time.

Here are examples of frugality in action. Meet Jenna, a teen who loves fashion but hates spending a fortune on clothes. She discovered thrift stores and now finds trendy, high-quality outfits for a fraction of the cost. By shopping second-hand, Jenna saves money and creates a unique wardrobe that stands out. And meet the Chin family, who reduced their grocery bills through meal planning and bulk buying. They create weekly meal plans, buy in bulk to save on staples, and use coupons to cut costs even further. These strategies not only save money but also reduce food waste.

REMEMBER:

Frugality is a powerful tool that can help you reach your financial goals faster while reducing waste and prioritizing quality. By comparing prices, using coupons, opting for second-hand items, and seeking value over the lowest price, you can make every dollar count. Embrace the art of frugality, and watch your savings grow while you enjoy the peace of mind that comes with smart spending.

6.2 SMART SHOPPING: TIPS FOR SAVVY CONSUMERS

You've saved up your hard-earned money, and now it's time to spend it wisely. Being a savvy consumer is crucial because it helps you avoid buyer's remorse and ensures you get the best value for your money. Imagine buying new tech only to find out a week later it's on sale for half the price. Ouch! Making informed purchasing decisions means doing a bit of homework before you hit the "buy" button.

One of the best strategies for smart shopping is researching products and reading reviews. Before you commit to a purchase, take some time to look up the product online. Websites like Amazon, Best Buy, and even YouTube have tons of reviews from real users. These reviews can give you insights into the product's quality, durability, and whether it lives up to the hype. It's like having a friend who's already tried it out and can give you the lowdown. By doing your homework, you can avoid wasting money on items that don't deliver.

Comparing prices across different stores is another smart move. Just because a product is available at your favorite store doesn't mean it's the best deal. Use price comparison websites and apps like Honey or PriceGrabber to check prices at various retailers. Sometimes, you can find the same product for much less elsewhere. Timing your purchases to take advantage of sales is also a game-changer. Many stores have seasonal sales, like back-to-school, Black Friday, or end-of-season clearances. If you can wait a little, you might score a great deal. Keep an eye out for these sales and plan your purchases accordingly.

Budgeting always plays a significant role in smart shopping. It's easy to get carried away when you see something you want, but sticking to a budget ensures you don't overspend. Start by setting spending limits for different categories. For instance, allocate a specific amount for clothes, tech, and entertainment. This way, you know exactly how much you can spend without derailing your financial goals. Allocating funds for necessary vs. discretionary purchases is also important. Prioritize your needs, like school supplies or a new pair of shoes, before splurging on wants like video games or concert tickets. This approach helps you stay focused and prevents impulse buying.

Take, for example, Ken, a teen who loves fashion but hates paying full price. He waits for seasonal sales to buy clothes. By planning his purchases around sales events like Black Friday or back-to-school, he scores trendy outfits without breaking the bank. Ken also uses price comparison apps to find the best deals. Before buying a new pair of Vans, he checks multiple stores and online platforms to ensure he's getting the best price. This habit has saved him a ton of money over the years.

Another smart shopper is Mia, who loves tech. She never buys the latest tech without reading reviews and comparing prices. Before purchasing a new phone, she spends hours watching YouTube or CNET reviews and reading user feedback on tech websites. She also waits for sales events, like Cyber Monday, to get the best deals. Her patience and research pay off, as she always ends up with high-quality tech at the best prices.

REMEMBER:

Being a savvy consumer isn't about depriving yourself; it's about making informed decisions that maximize your money's value. By researching products, comparing prices, and sticking to a budget, you can avoid buyer's remorse and enjoy your purchases guilt-free. So, the next time you're about to make a purchase, take a moment to do a little homework. Your wallet—and your future self—will thank you.

6.3 AVOIDING IMPULSE BUYS: STAYING FOCUSED ON YOUR GOALS

Impulse buying is like that sneaky friend who always convinces you to do something you later regret. It's when you purchase something on a whim, without planning or considering the consequences. Imagine walking past a store, seeing shiny new tech, and buying it immediately, only to realize later that you didn't really need it. The consequences of impulse buying can be pretty rough. Financial strain is a big one. Spending money impulsively can leave you broke before your next allowance or paycheck, making it hard to cover essentials. You also end up accumulating unnecessary items that clutter your space and drain your wallet. Plus, there's the guilt and buyer's remorse. Ever bought something and felt a wave of regret wash over you? That's the aftermath of an impulse buy.

So how do you avoid falling into the impulse buy trap? Start by creating a shopping list and sticking to it. Before you go shopping, make a list of what you need and promise yourself you'll only buy those items. This keeps you focused and reduces the temptation to buy things on a whim. Another effective strategy is implementing a **cooling-off** period. If you see something you really want, wait 24 hours before making the purchase. This gives you time to think about whether you truly need it and can afford it. Often, the urge to buy will pass, saving you money and regret.

Setting specific financial goals can also help curb impulse spending. When you have clear goals, like saving for a new bike or a trip, you're more likely to think twice before spending on unnecessary items. These goals act as a constant reminder of what you're working towards and make it easier to resist the temptation of impulse buys. Using cash instead of cards is another trick. When you pay with cash, you physically see the money leaving your wallet, making you more mindful of your spending. This tactile experience can help you stick to your budget and avoid impulsive purchases.

The psychology behind impulse buying is fascinating. Instant gratification plays a huge role. We live in a world where we want things now, and waiting feels like torture. Buying something instantly satisfies that urge, but the pleasure is often short-lived. Peer pressure and social influences also contribute. Your friends might be buying the latest techs or trendy clothes, and you feel the need to keep up. Marketing tactics in stores are designed to trigger impulse buys too. Ever notice those tempting items near the checkout counter? They're strategically placed to catch your eye and make you reach for your wallet.

REMEMBER:

Avoiding impulse buys is all about staying focused on your goals and being mindful of your spending. By creating a shopping list, implementing a cooling-off period, setting financial goals, and using cash, you can resist the urge to buy on a whim. Understanding the psychology behind impulse buying and recognizing the tactics used to lure you into spending can also empower you to make better choices. So, the next time you feel the urge to splurge, take a moment to pause and consider the long-term benefits of staying focused on your financial goals.

6.4 UNDERSTANDING ADVERTISING: HOW TO RESIST MARKETING TRICKS

Ever wondered why you suddenly crave a burger right after seeing a commercial or why you can't stop thinking about that shiny new tech after watching an influencer rave about it? That's the magic of advertising at work. Advertisers know exactly how to push your buttons, using various techniques to persuade you to buy their products. Emotional appeals are one of their favorite tools. They tug at your heartstrings, making you feel happy, sad, or excited, all to associate those feelings with their product. Think of those touching commercials showing friends having the time of their lives with a particular brand of soda. It's designed to make you think that soda equals friendship and fun.

Limited-time offers create a sense of urgency that's hard to resist. You've seen the flashing "Only 24 hours left!" banners, right? They make you feel like you'll miss out on something amazing if you don't act now. It's all about **FOMO—Fear of Missing Out**. Celebrity endorsements are another powerful tactic. When you see your favorite singer or actor using a product, it feels like a personal recommendation. If it's good enough for them, it must be good enough for you, right? Product placement in media is more subtle but just as effective. Ever notice how characters in movies or TV shows always seem to be using particular brands? It's not a coincidence. It's strategic advertising designed to blend seamlessly into the content you love.

So how do you navigate this minefield of marketing tricks? Start by questioning the necessity of the product. Do you really need it, or is it just the clever advertising talking? Next, do some research. Look up alternative products and read reviews. You might find a better, more affordable option. Recognizing and resisting emotional manipulation is crucial. Just because an ad makes you feel a certain way doesn't mean you need the product. Take a step back and evaluate the real value it adds to your life.

And please be aware, digital and social media advertising takes these tactics to a whole new level. Sponsored content on social media is everywhere. Influencers get paid to promote products, often making it hard to tell genuine recommendations from paid promotions. Targeted ads based on your browsing history follow you around online, making it seem like the universe is telling you to buy that new pair of shoes. Influencer marketing leverages the trust and connection you feel with social media personalities to persuade you to buy products they endorse. It's like getting a recommendation from a friend, but it's important to remember that influencers are often paid for their endorsements.

Jeremiah is an example of a savvy teen who saw an ad for a new skincare product while scrolling through Instagram. Instead of buying it on impulse, he did some research. He read reviews, compared it with other products, and even checked out YouTube videos. In the end, he found a better product at a lower price. Then there's Jeff, who has become a pro at recognizing "clickbait" advertisements. Whenever he sees those too-good-to-be-true offers, he ignores them and does his homework. This habit has saved him from wasting money on products that don't live up to the hype.

REMEMBER:

Advertising is designed to influence you, but you have the power to make informed decisions. By questioning the necessity of products, researching alternatives, and recognizing emotional manipulation, you can resist marketing tricks and make purchases based on value, not persuasion. Understanding how digital advertising targets you and learning to navigate it can also help you become a more mindful consumer. So next time you see an ad that makes you want to buy something instantly, take a moment to pause and think. Your wallet—and your future self—will thank you.

CHAPTER 7
CREDIT AND DEBT MANAGEMENT

> *"The man who never has money enough to pay his debts has too much of something else."*

E ver tried juggling? Imagine doing it with flaming torches while riding a unicycle. That's what managing credit and debt can feel like if you don't know what you're doing. But don't worry, I'm here to help you turn those flaming torches into harmless, manageable beanbags. Let's dive into the world of credit and debt, where you'll learn to juggle your finances like a pro, without getting burned.

7.1 WHAT IS CREDIT? THE BASICS FOR TEENS

So, what exactly is credit? At its core, credit is the ability to borrow money with the promise to repay it later. Think of it as a financial IOU. Whether you're swiping a credit card at your favorite store or taking out a loan for college, you're essentially borrowing money that you'll pay back over time. Credit is crucial for purchasing large items like a car or a house, things you probably can't pay for all at once. Instead of saving for years, you can buy now and pay later, as long as you keep up with your payments.

There are various types of credit, each serving different purposes. Credit cards are probably the most familiar. They allow you to borrow money up to a certain limit and pay it back either in full each month or over time with "interest". Then there are student loans, which help cover the costs of your education. These loans often come with lower interest rates and somewhat more flexible repayment terms, making them more manageable. Personal loans are another option, giving you a lump sum of money to use for anything from consolidating debt to funding a big purchase. Lastly, store credit is specific to certain retailers, letting you buy now and pay later for items from that store. Each type of credit has pros and cons, and understanding them can help you make smarter financial decisions.

Using credit comes with both benefits and risks. One of the biggest advantages is building a credit history. Your credit history is like a financial report card that shows lenders how responsible you are with borrowed money. A good credit history can open doors to lower interest rates on loans and better deals on credit cards. Credit also offers the convenience of not carrying cash. Imagine you're out with friends and spot something you really want to buy but don't have enough cash on hand. A credit card can save the day, as long as you can pay it off later.

But beware, credit can be a double-edged sword. The risk of accumulating debt is very real. If you're not careful, it's easy to spend more than you can repay, leading to high-interest debt that can spiral out of control. Mismanaging credit can hurt your credit score, making it harder to get loans or even rent an apartment in the future. It's like eating too much candy—you enjoy it now but regret it later when you're dealing with cavities.

Let's look at some real-life examples to illustrate these points. Imagine you're on a road trip, and your car breaks down in the middle of nowhere. Using a credit card to cover the emergency repair can get you back on the road without draining your savings. This is a smart use of credit. On the flip side, let's say you get a credit card and start using it for everything—clothes, techs, dining out. Before you know it, you've maxed out your limit and can't afford to pay off the balance. The high-interest debt starts piling up, and you're stuck in a financial rut. This is the downside of mismanaging credit.

REMEMBER:

Credit is a powerful tool that can help you achieve your financial goals, but it requires responsible handling. Understanding the basics of credit, the types available, and the potential benefits and risks can set you on the path to smart financial management. **Credit isn't free money!** It's a loan you'll need to repay, often with interest. Use it wisely, and it can be a valuable ally in your financial journey.

And please, please, I can't stress this point enough. If you learn nothing more from this book, learn the above. Credit can be great in an emergency and planned large purchases when you don't have sufficient funds. But it can be like an illegal drug if it's not managed! When your credit score is damaged, all of the goals and savings processes we are discussing become a challenge to achieve. And that word again, **Stress** raises its ugly head, so be disciplined and properly manage your credit use. More on this below...

7.2 BUILDING GOOD CREDIT: STEPS TO GET STARTED

Establishing good credit habits early on is like planting seeds for a fruitful financial future. Imagine trying to get a loan for your dream car or your first apartment. Without a solid credit history, you might face higher interest rates or even get turned down. Building good credit as a teen can make life so much easier down the road. Easier approval for loans, lower interest rates on credit cards, and even better insurance premiums are all benefits of having a good credit score. Think of it as setting yourself up for a financial VIP pass.

So, how do you start building good credit? One simple way is by opening a student or secured credit card. These cards are designed for people who are new to credit and often come with lower credit limits and more manageable terms. For example, a secured credit card requires a deposit that serves as your credit limit. It's like training wheels for your financial life, helping you build credit without the risk of overspending. Once you have a card, make small, manageable purchases. Buy things you would normally pay cash for, like gas or groceries, and **then pay off the balance in full each month**. This shows lenders that you're responsible and can manage credit effectively. Avoid making large purchases that you can't pay off immediately, as this can lead to debt and hurt your credit score.

Paying off your balance in full each month is crucial. Not only does this prevent you from accumulating debt, but it also positively impacts your credit score. Late payments can be a credit killer. Even one missed payment can ding your score significantly. Set up automatic payments to ensure you never miss a due date. Most banks and credit card companies offer this service, and it's a lifesaver for those of us who might be a bit forgetful.

Now, let's talk about credit utilization. This is the ratio of your credit card balance to your credit limit, and it plays a big role in determining your credit score. Keeping your credit card balances low relative to your credit limit shows that you're not relying too heavily on credit. For example, if you have a credit card with a $1,000 limit, try to keep your balance below $300. Using only $200 of that limit is even better. The lower your credit utilization, the more favorably it reflects on your credit report.

Maintaining good credit habits is an ongoing process. Regularly reviewing your credit reports helps you catch errors and monitor your progress. You can get a free credit report from **AnnualCreditReport.com** once a year from each of the three major credit bureaus. It's like getting a report card for your finances, and it's crucial to check for any inaccuracies. If you spot an error, report it immediately to get it corrected. Avoiding unnecessary credit inquiries is also important. Each time you apply for credit, it results in a hard inquiry, which can temporarily lower your score. Only apply for credit when you need it and avoid opening multiple accounts in a short period.

Another tip is to set up alerts that notify you of any changes to your credit report. Many financial apps and services offer this feature for free. It keeps you in the loop and allows you to act quickly if something seems off. Being proactive about your credit can save you a lot of headaches down the line. Also, consider using budgeting apps to manage your finances better. Apps like Mint or YNAB can help you track your spending, set savings goals, and make sure you're not overspending, which indirectly helps maintain good credit.

REMEMBER:

Building good credit as a teen sets the stage for a financially secure future. It's about making smart choices, being responsible, and staying informed. By opening a student or secured credit card, making small purchases, paying off the balance in full, and keeping your credit utilization low, you're laying the groundwork for excellent credit. Regularly review your credit reports, set up automatic payments, and avoid unnecessary credit inquiries to maintain these good habits.

7.3 UNDERSTANDING CREDIT SCORES: WHAT THEY MEAN AND WHY THEY MATTER

Your credit score is like your financial GPA. Just like in school, where your grades reflect your academic performance, your credit score is a numerical representation of your creditworthiness. Ranging typically from 300 to 850, this score helps lenders and creditors decide how risky it is to lend you money. A higher score means you're viewed as a responsible borrower, while a lower score might make lenders think twice. It's calculated based on several factors, each playing a crucial role in painting a picture of your financial habits.

Payment history is the superstar of credit scores. It accounts for the largest portion, about 35%, of your score. Simply put, lenders want to know if you pay your bills on time. Late payments, missed payments, or defaults can significantly ding your score. Next up is the credit utilization ratio, which is the amount of credit you're using compared to your total available credit. This factor contributes about 30% to your score. If you're maxing out your cards, it signals to lenders that you might be overextended, even if you're making payments on time. Keeping this ratio low, ideally below 30%, can help boost your score.

Length of credit history is another important piece of the puzzle, making up about 15% of your score. Lenders like to see a long track record of responsible credit use. If you're new to credit, you won't have much history, but that's okay. Starting early and maintaining good habits will build this over time. Then there are the types of credit used, which account for 10% of your score. A mix of credit types, like credit cards, installment loans, and retail accounts, shows lenders that you can handle different kinds of credit responsibly. Lastly, recent credit inquiries contribute about 10%. Each time you apply for credit, it results in a hard inquiry on your credit report. Too many inquiries in a short period can lower your score, as it might suggest you're desperate for credit.

So why does a good credit score matter? For starters, it can save you a lot of money in the long run. Better interest rates on loans and credit cards are one of the biggest perks. Imagine applying for a car loan. With a high credit score, you might secure a loan with a lower interest rate, saving you hundreds or even thousands of dollars over the life of the loan. Easier approval for renting an apartment is another benefit. Landlords often check credit scores to ensure potential tenants are financially responsible. A good score can make the difference between landing your dream apartment or continuing the search. Lower insurance premiums are also tied to your credit score. Insurance companies use your score to assess risk, and a higher score can lead to lower premiums on auto and home insurance. **And now more and more companies are reviewing a potential new hire's credit report to evaluate discipline and financial responsibility**. Nuff said!

As said, regularly reviewing your credit report helps you stay on top of your financial health. Set a reminder to check your report at least once a year. Look for any discrepancies or unfamiliar accounts that could indicate identity theft. Setting up automatic payments for your bills ensures you never miss a due date, which helps maintain a positive payment history. Avoid unnecessary credit inquiries by only applying for credit when you need it. Each hard inquiry can shave a few points off your score, so it's best to be strategic about when and why you're applying for new credit.

Here is further background:

Understanding Your Credit Report

When you apply for credit, the company from whom you're requesting it will check your credit report from one or more of the major consumer reporting agencies: TransUnion®, Equifax®, or Experian®. Each agency's report may look different, but they contain the same information:

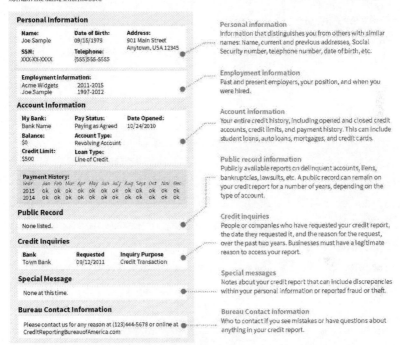

Personal Information

Name:	Date of Birth:	Address:
Joe Sample	09/15/1979	901 Main Street
SSN:	Telephone:	Anytown, USA 12345
XXX-XX-XXXX	(555)555-5555	

Employment information:

Acme Widgets	2011-2015
Joe Sample	1997-2012

Account Information

My Bank:	Pay Status:	Date Opened:
Bank Name	Paying as Agreed	10/24/2010
Balance:	Account Type:	
$0	Revolving Account	
Credit Limit:	Loan Type:	
$500	Line of Credit	

Payment History:

Year	Jan	Feb	Mar	Apr	May	Jun	July	Aug	Sept	Oct	Nov	Dec
2015	ok	ok	ok	ok	ok	ok	ok	ok	ok	ok	ok	ok
2014	ok	ok	ok	ok	ok	ok	ok	ok	ok	ok	ok	ok

Public Record

None listed.

Credit Inquiries

Bank	Requested	Inquiry Purpose
Town Bank	09/12/2011	Credit Transaction

Special Message

None at this time.

Bureau Contact Information

Please contact us for any reason at (123)444-5678 or online at CreditReportingBureauofAmerica.com

Personal information — Information that distinguishes you from others with similar names: Name, current and previous addresses, Social Security number, telephone number, date of birth, etc.

Employment information — Past and present employers, your position, and when you were hired.

Account information — Your entire credit history, including opened and closed credit accounts, credit limits, and payment history. This can include student loans, auto loans, mortgages, and credit cards.

Public record information — Publicly available reports on delinquent accounts, liens, bankruptcies, lawsuits, etc. A public record can remain on your credit report for a number of years, depending on the type of account.

Credit inquiries — People or companies who have requested your credit report, the date they requested it, and the reason for the request, over the past two years. Businesses must have a legitimate reason to access your report.

Special messages — Notes about your credit report that can include discrepancies within your personal information or reported fraud or theft.

Bureau Contact information — Who to contact if you see mistakes or have questions about anything in your credit report.

Review your credit report annually to make sure there are no mistakes. This is especially important when you're considering an action that may require a loan, like purchasing a house, buying or leasing a car, and/or applying for a student loan. Request a free copy of your credit report each year from **AnnualCreditReport.com**.

7.4 AVOIDING DEBT: TIPS TO STAY DEBT-FREE

I hope you are noting and taking to heart my **"Danger, Danger"** (ask your parents or look up this "Lost in Space" reference) messages in this chapter regarding credit. And the same holds true regarding debt.

Imagine this: you're finally out on your own, ready to conquer the world, but then you get hit with a mountain of bills you can't pay. That's the nightmare of accumulating debt. The first thing to understand is that debt isn't just about owing money; it's about the high-interest payments that come with it. These payments can quickly spiral out of control, making it feel like you're throwing money into a black hole. Interest adds up fast, and before you know it, you're paying off the interest instead of the actual debt. This can lead to stress and financial strain, impacting not just your wallet but your mental health too. The constant worry about how you'll make ends meet can take a toll, making it hard to focus on anything else.

The impact of debt on your future financial opportunities is another big issue. Imagine wanting to buy your first car or even your dream house, only to find out your poor credit score makes it impossible to get a loan. Or maybe you get approved, but the interest rates are so high that you're paying way more than you should. Debt can also affect your ability to rent an apartment or even get a job, as many employers now check credit scores as part of their hiring process. In short, debt can close doors you didn't even know were open.

So, how do you avoid falling into this trap? Start by living within your means. This might sound simple, but it's often easier said than done. It means spending less than you earn and avoiding the temptation to splurge on things you don't really need. One way to do this, as I've said, is by making a budget and sticking to it. Allocate your funds for essential expenses like rent, groceries, and utilities first. Then, set aside money for savings. Whatever's left can go towards fun stuff like eating out or buying new clothes. This way, you ensure that your basic needs are covered, and you're also building a financial cushion for the future.

Avoiding unnecessary credit card use is another crucial strategy. Credit cards can be useful tools, but they can also lead to trouble if not used responsibly. It's easy to swipe now and worry about paying later, but this mindset can quickly lead to debt. Use your credit card only for planned expenses that you know you can pay off in full when the bill comes. This helps you avoid interest charges and keeps your debt under control. If you're tempted to use your credit card for impulse purchases, leave it at home and carry cash instead. Seeing the money leave your wallet can make you think twice about spending it.

As I've also said, building an emergency fund is another smart move. Life is full of surprises, and not all of them are good. Having an emergency fund means you have money set aside for unexpected expenses like medical bills or car repairs. This fund acts as a financial safety net, so you don't have to rely on credit cards or loans when something unexpected happens. Aim to save at least three to six months' worth of living expenses in your emergency fund. Start small if you need to, but make it a habit to contribute regularly. Even a few dollars each week can add up over time.

To make the point, consider the following examples. Laquita is a college student who managed to avoid student loans by applying for scholarships and working part-time throughout her studies. She graduated debt-free, giving her a head start in her career without the burden of loan repayments. Or consider Matt, a young adult who used budgeting apps like **Mint** to manage his expenses. By tracking his spending, he was able to cut down on unnecessary costs and save more, avoiding the need to rely on credit. These stories show that with a bit of planning and discipline, it's entirely possible to stay debt-free and financially secure.

Avoiding debt is about making smart financial choices and planning for the future. By living within your means, avoiding unnecessary credit card use, and building an emergency fund, you can protect yourself from the pitfalls of debt. Remember, the goal is to enjoy financial freedom without the stress and limitations that debt brings.

7.5 IF YOU'RE IN DEBT: STRATEGIES FOR PAYING IT OFF

Finding yourself in debt can feel like trying to climb out of a deep hole with nothing but a spoon. It's overwhelming and stressful, but with the right approach, you can dig your way out. The first step is to assess your debt situation. Grab a notebook, open a spreadsheet, or use a tool in a banking app to list all your debts. Include the amount owed, the interest rate, and the minimum monthly payment for each one. This gives you a clear picture of what you're dealing with. Prioritize high-interest debts first, as these are the ones that cost you the most over time. For example, if you have a credit card with a 20% interest rate and a student loan with a 5% rate, focus on paying off the credit card first.

Once you've assessed your debt, it's time to choose a repayment strategy. One popular method is the **Snowball method**. This involves paying off your smallest debts first while making minimum payments on the larger ones. The idea is to gain momentum as you eliminate smaller debts, which can be incredibly motivating. Picture it like rolling a snowball down a hill that gets bigger and faster as it goes. Another approach is the **Avalanche method**, where you focus on paying off the debts with the highest interest rates first. This can save you more money in the long run, although it might take longer to see progress compared to the snowball method. Consolidation loans are another option, allowing you to combine multiple debts into one loan with a lower interest rate. This simplifies your payments and can potentially reduce your overall interest costs.

Communicating with creditors is a crucial but often overlooked step in managing debt. If you're struggling to make payments, don't hide from your creditors. Reach out to them and explain your situation. Many creditors are willing to negotiate lower interest rates or set up payment plans to help you manage your debt more effectively. It's in their best interest to work with you rather than see you default. For instance, you might be able to lower your credit card interest rate from 20% to 15%, which can make a significant difference in your monthly payments. Setting up a payment plan can also spread out your debt over a longer period, making it more manageable.

Staying motivated during debt repayment is essential for success. It can be a long and challenging process, but keeping your spirits high can make all the difference. Celebrate small victories along the way. Did you pay off one of your smaller debts? Treat yourself to something small, like a movie night. These little rewards can keep you motivated and remind you that you're making progress. Keeping track of your progress visually can also be helpful. Create a chart or use an app to see how much you've paid off and how much you have left. Watching your debt decrease can be incredibly satisfying and motivating.

Setting realistic milestones and goals is another way to stay focused. Break down your overall debt into smaller, achievable targets. For example, if you have $10,000 in debt, aim to pay off $1,000 in the next three months. Meeting these smaller goals can give you a sense of accomplishment and keep you on track. Remember, the journey to being debt-free is a marathon, not a sprint. It's about consistent, steady progress rather than quick fixes.

REMEMBER:

If you're in debt, start by assessing your situation, choosing a repayment strategy, communicating with creditors, and staying motivated. And always understand that managing credit and debt is a crucial part of financial health.

Next, we'll explore how to make your money work for you.

CHAPTER 8
INTRODUCTION TO INVESTING

> *"The best time to plant a tree was 20 years ago. The second-best time is now."*

CHINESE PROVERB

Picture this: you're at the fair, and you see a booth offering a game where you can win a giant stuffed panda. You pay a small fee, and if you play your cards right, you walk away with a prize much bigger than what you paid. Investing is a bit like that game, but instead of a stuffed panda, you have the potential to grow your money over time. With research and effort, investing can be a valuable ticket to financial success.

8.1 INVESTING 101: THE BASICS YOU NEED TO KNOW

So, what exactly is investing? At its core, investing is the act of putting your money into assets that have the potential to grow in value over time. Think of it as planting a seed in a garden. With the right care and conditions, that seed can grow into a flourishing plant, producing fruit or flowers that you can enjoy. The goal of investing is to generate a return on investment (**ROI**), which means making more money than you initially put in. This growth can come from various sources, such as dividends from stocks, interest from bonds, or growth in the value of the stock itself.

Now, you might be wondering, how is investing different from saving? It's a great question, and understanding the distinction is key to building a solid financial foundation. Saving is all about setting aside money for shorter-term goals and emergencies. It's like having a piggy bank that you can dip into when you need cash quickly, like for a new phone or an unexpected expense. Investing, on the other hand, is geared towards long-term growth. It involves taking some level of **Risk** (and a much higher risk than savings) with the expectation of higher returns over time. For example, while saving might help you buy a new phone next month, investing can help you fund your college education or even retire comfortably one day.

To get a clearer picture, let's dive into some basic investment terms. First up is **risk and return**. Risk refers to the potential of losing some or all of your investment, while return is the profit you gain. Higher risk often comes with the possibility of higher returns, but it can also mean bigger losses. Next is **diversification**, which means spreading your investments across different assets to reduce risk. Imagine not putting all your eggs in one basket; if one basket drops, you still have others intact. Then there's your **portfolio**, which is simply the collection of all your investments. Finally, we have **asset classes**, which are categories of investments like stocks, bonds, and real estate. Each asset class has different characteristics and levels of risk and return.

The stock market can seem like a mysterious place, but it's actually quite straightforward once you break it down. When you buy shares of a company, you're essentially buying a small piece of that company. If the company does well, the value of your shares can increase, and you might even receive dividends, which are a portion of the company's profits. Stock exchanges, such as **the New York Stock Exchange (NYSE) and NASDAQ**, are platforms where these shares are bought and sold. Companies like Apple, Amazon, and Google are traded on these exchanges, and their stock prices can fluctuate based on various factors, including company performance and market conditions.

Investing is really about making informed decisions and understanding the basics. With the right knowledge, experience, and a bit of patience, you can turn your investments into a powerful tool for building wealth over time. So, the next time you think about your financial future, remember that investing is like planting that seed in your garden. With the right care, it can grow into something beautiful and fruitful.

8.2 SIMPLE INVESTMENTS FOR TEENS: STOCKS, BONDS, AND MUTUAL FUNDS

Imagine you're at the mall, and you decide to buy a piece of your favorite store. Sounds wild, right? Well, that's essentially what you're doing when you buy stocks. When you purchase a stock, you're buying a small piece of a company, making you a part-owner. This ownership means you get to share in the company's profits through dividends, and if the company grows, the value of your shares can increase. Think about owning a slice of Disney—every time a new Marvel movie breaks box office records, your piece of the pie gets a little bit sweeter.

Bonds might sound a bit more boring, but they play a crucial role in any investment portfolio. When you buy a bond, you're essentially **lending money** to a company or the government. In return, they promise to pay you back with interest over a set period. It's like being the bank. For example, U.S. Treasury bonds are considered very safe because they are backed by the United States government. The interest payments you receive are like a steady paycheck, providing a reliable income stream with less risk compared to stocks.

Then there are mutual funds, which are like a buffet of investments. Instead of buying individual stocks or bonds, you pool your money with other investors to buy a diversified portfolio managed by a professional fund manager. This expert picks a mix of assets to help balance risk and return. Imagine investing in a mutual fund that includes tech stocks, healthcare companies, and some bonds. This diversification can help reduce risk because if one investment doesn't perform well, others might offset the loss. You benefit from the expertise of the fund manager, who makes informed decisions to grow the fund's value.

Choosing between these investment options can feel like standing in front of a candy store with too many delicious choices. How do you decide? Start by considering your **risk tolerance**. Are you okay with seeing your investment value go up and down, or do you prefer more stability? Stocks can offer high returns but come with higher risk. Bonds are more stable but usually offer lower returns. Mutual funds provide a balanced approach, combining stocks and bonds to spread out risk.

Next, evaluate your investment goals. Are you saving for something short-term or a long-term goal like college or retirement? If you're thinking long-term, stocks might be a good option because they have the potential for significant growth over time. For more immediate needs, bonds might be a safer bet. Mutual funds can fit into both categories depending on their composition.

Diversifying across different types of assets is also crucial. Don't put all your eggs in one basket. By spreading your investments across stocks, bonds, and mutual funds, you can balance potential risks and rewards. This way, if one investment underperforms, others in your portfolio can help cushion the blow.

To put this into perspective, let's consider a simple exercise. Imagine you have $1,000 to invest. You might decide to put $400 into a tech stock like Apple, $300 into U.S. Treasury bonds, and the remaining $300 into a diversified mutual fund. Over time, the stock might experience significant growth, the bonds provide steady interest payments, and the mutual fund offers a balanced return. This diversified approach helps you manage risk while aiming for growth.

Investing doesn't have to be complicated or intimidating. Understanding the basics of stocks, bonds, and mutual funds and how they fit into your financial goals can set you on the path to financial success. Remember, it's not about making a quick buck but about growing your wealth over time.

8.3 UNDERSTANDING COMPOUND INTEREST: YOU AND YOUR MONEY'S BEST FRIEND

Imagine you've got a small snowball, and you start rolling it down a hill. At first, it picks up just a little bit of snow, but as it keeps rolling, it gathers more and more, growing bigger and faster. That's what compound interest does to your money. Unlike simple interest, which only earns interest on your initial deposit, compound interest earns interest on both your initial amount and the interest that accumulates over time. It's like a snowball effect for your savings. For instance, if you put money into a savings account with compound interest, not only does your original deposit earn interest, but the interest you earn also starts earning interest. It's a powerful way to grow your money over time.

The magic of compound interest lies in its exponential growth potential. The longer you let your money sit, the more it grows, and the growth accelerates over time.

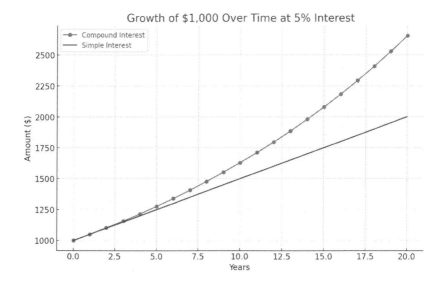

Here's a visual comparison of how $1,000 grows over time with compound interest (green line) at a 5% rate versus simple interest (blue line). You can see that as time goes on, the gap between compound interest and simple interest widens significantly. This demonstrates the power of compound interest, which builds on both the initial investment and the accumulated interest, whereas simple interest grows only on the initial investment.

The earlier you start, the more time your money has to grow. Starting to invest as a teen gives you a significant advantage, allowing you to maximize the benefits of compounding over a longer period.

8.4 STARTING SMALL: INVESTING WITH LIMITED FUNDS

Imagine standing in front of a skyscraper and wondering how it got so tall. The truth is, it started with just one brick. Investing is a lot like that. You don't need a mountain of cash to get started. Even small amounts can grow into something substantial over time. Micro-investing platforms like **Acorns** and **Stash** are perfect for teens who want to dip their toes into the investment world. These apps allow you to invest spare change from everyday purchases, making it easy to start small. Fractional shares also make it possible to buy pieces of high-value stocks. For instance, you could invest just $5 in a stock like Amazon, which might otherwise seem out of reach.

Gathering funds to start investing might seem challenging, but with a little creativity, it's entirely doable. Consider saving a portion of your allowance or job earnings. Even setting aside $10 a week can add up over time. Another fun way to build your investment funds is by participating in investment challenges. Challenge yourself to save a certain amount by a specific date and reward yourself when you achieve it. You could also pool resources with friends for a group investment, turning it into a shared learning experience. The key is to be consistent and disciplined, making saving a regular habit.

User-friendly investment apps can be a game-changer, especially for beginners. **Robinhood** is one such app that offers commission-free trading and an easy-to-use interface. It's a great way to start investing without worrying about trading fees eating into your profits. Another excellent option is **M1 Finance**, which combines the best of robo-advisory services with hands-on control. You can create a diversified portfolio tailored to your goals and risk tolerance. Setting up an account on these apps is straightforward. For example, with a micro-investing app, you can start by linking your bank account, setting your investment preferences, and letting the app do the rest. It's like having a personal financial advisor in your pocket.

When you're just starting out, having access to the right tools and resources can make a huge difference. Fortunately, there are a few great platforms designed with young investors in mind that offer educational content to guide you along the way. For example, **Public** and **Fidelity Youth Account** are excellent options for younger audiences. These platforms not only give you the ability to invest in stocks and ETFs with no commission fees but also provide educational content tailored to beginners.

The **Public** app offers a social aspect where you can follow experienced investors, learn from their strategies, and even ask questions. It's a fun way to start your investing journey while picking up valuable tips and advice from others. On the other hand, **Fidelity Youth Account** is geared toward teens and comes with access to financial literacy tools and content to help you understand the basics of investing, budgeting, and saving.

Both platforms make it easy to get started, even with a small amount of money, while helping you build financial confidence. Whether you're looking for a hands-on investing experience with educational content or simply want to start learning about how the stock market works, these accounts are a great steppingstone toward financial independence.

Let's look at success stories. There's a teen who started with just $20, investing in fractional shares through an app. Over time, by consistently adding small amounts, the portfolio grew significantly. This teen learned the ropes of investing without needing a large initial sum. Another example is using spare change to invest. Imagine rounding up your coffee purchase from $3.75 to $4.00, with the extra $0.25 going into your investment account. It might seem like a small amount, but over weeks and months, it can grow into a nice sum. These examples show that you don't need a lot of money to start investing; you just need to start.

With apps like the above, you can invest small amounts, learning valuable financial skills along the way. Imagine growing your portfolio from just a few dollars into something much larger, all while gaining confidence and knowledge in the world of investing.

8.5 AVOIDING INVESTMENT SCAMS: STAYING SAFE

Imagine you're at a carnival or at the beach and a guy in a flashy suit promises you a guaranteed win if you play his game. It sounds too good to be true, right? That's what investment scams are like—shiny promises with a high risk of losing your money. Recognizing and avoiding scams is crucial because falling for one can be financially devastating and emotionally draining. Remember, if it sounds too good to be true, it probably is.

Investment scams come in various forms, but they share common characteristics. Watch out for schemes that guarantee huge returns with no risk or pressure you to act quickly. Fraudsters often use persuasive language and flashy presentations to create a sense of urgency. They might also be vague about how the investment works, avoiding detailed explanations.

The financial and emotional impact of falling for a scam can be severe. Not only can you lose your hard-earned money, but the stress and embarrassment can take a toll on your mental health.

It's essential to be cautious and diligent when evaluating investment opportunities.

To identify legitimate investment opportunities, start by thoroughly researching the investment. Look for information about the company or person offering the investment. Check for regulatory approval, such as registration with the Securities and Exchange Commission (**SEC**) in the U.S., or equivalent bodies in other countries. Legitimate investments will have clear, transparent information available. Be wary of red flags, such as unsolicited offers, especially those received via email or social media. **Scammers often use high-pressure tactics to rush you into a decision without giving you time to think it through.** Always take your time and don't let anyone push you into an investment.

The role of **Financial Advisors** and mentors can't be overstated when it comes to avoiding scams. Consulting with a financial advisor can provide professional insights and advice tailored to your financial situation. Advisors can help you understand the risks and benefits of different investments, guiding you toward safer options. Learning from experienced investors can also be valuable. They've likely encountered various scams and can share their knowledge on how to spot and avoid them. Building a network of trusted sources can significantly reduce your risk of falling victim to fraud.

Here is a real-life example. **Ponzi** schemes are a classic type of fraud where returns are paid to earlier investors using the capital (money) from newer investors, rather than from profit earned. Eventually, the scheme collapses when there aren't enough new investors to pay returns. A famous example is Bernie Madoff's Ponzi scheme, which defrauded investors (some very famous) of billions of dollars. Fake investment websites are another common scam. These sites often look professional and legitimate but are set up to steal your money. Always verify the legitimacy of a website by checking for reviews and regulatory information.

Phishing attempts are another tactic used by scammers. They typically involve fraudulent emails or messages that appear to come from reputable sources, asking for personal information or prompting you to click on malicious links. Recognizing and reporting a phishing attempt is crucial. If you receive an email claiming to be from your bank or an investment firm asking for sensitive information, don't click on any links. Instead, contact the institution directly using a verified phone number or email address to confirm the authenticity of the request.

As you navigate the world of investing, staying safe from scams is vital. By recognizing the common characteristics of fraudulent schemes, thoroughly researching investments, consulting with trusted advisors, and learning from real-life examples, you can protect yourself from financial and emotional harm.

REMEMBER:

Investing offers great opportunities for building a secure financial future, but it's essential to navigate the process wisely. By understanding the basics, exploring different types of investments, leveraging the power of compound interest, starting small, and staying vigilant against scams, you're setting yourself up for success. Remember, investing is about growing your wealth over time, not chasing quick, risky returns. Stay vigilant, be cautious, and always trust your instincts.

In the next chapter, we'll dive into financial responsibility and ethics, ensuring your investment journey aligns with your values and long-term goals.

CHAPTER 9
FINANCIAL RESPONSIBILITY AND ETHICS

66 *"Money is a tool. Used properly, it makes something beautiful; used wrong, it makes a mess!"*

BRADLEY VINSON

66 *"A good reputation is more valuable than money."*

PUBLILIUS SYRUS

I magine you're at your favorite coffee shop, and the barista accidentally gives you extra change. It's not a huge amount, but it's enough to make you pause. Do you keep it and walk away, or do you return it? This small scenario is a perfect example of the ethical decisions we face every day. Whether it's dealing with money, making purchases, or managing our finances, ethics plays a huge role in how we handle these situations.

9.1 THE ETHICS OF MONEY: MAKING RESPONSIBLE CHOICES

So, what does it mean to make ethical financial choices? At its core, ethical financial behavior revolves around a few key principles: honesty, fairness, accountability, and transparency. These principles guide our decisions and actions, ensuring that we handle our finances in a way that's not just good for us but also fair and just for others.

Honesty in financial transactions means being truthful about your financial dealings. This could be as simple as honestly reporting all your income on your tax returns or not hiding expenses to make your budget look better than it is. Fairness in dealings involves treating others as you would want to be treated. If you're selling something, make sure it's priced fairly and that you're not taking advantage of the buyer. Accountability for financial decisions means taking responsibility for your choices, whether they lead to success or failure. If you make a bad investment, own up to it and learn from the mistake instead of blaming others. Lastly, transparency in financial matters means being open and clear about your financial situation. This could involve discussing financial goals and challenges with your family or being upfront about the costs of a project you're working on.

Integrity is crucial when handling money. It's what keeps you from cutting corners or engaging in dishonest practices. Avoiding dishonest practices might seem obvious, but it's easier said than done. Imagine you find a loophole that allows you to dodge a small tax payment. It might seem like a win in the short term, but it's dishonest and can lead to bigger problems down the road. Ensuring transparent record-keeping is another aspect of integrity. This means keeping accurate and honest records of your financial transactions. Whether it's your personal budget or a business ledger, transparency helps build trust and ensures that you're always on solid ground. For example, always report all your income accurately on your tax returns. It might be tempting to underreport to save a few bucks, but honesty is always the best policy.

Ethical dilemmas in finance are situations where you must choose between what's easy and what's right. Imagine you're offered a high-paying job at a company known for unethical practices. The pay is tempting, but the company's reputation makes you uncomfortable. Do you take the job for the money, or do you turn it down and look for something more aligned with your values?

Navigating these ethical dilemmas can be tricky, but there are strategies to help you make the right choice. Consulting with mentors or advisors can provide valuable perspectives and guidance. Reflecting on the long-term consequences of your decisions is also important. What might seem like a small, insignificant choice now could have major repercussions later.

One way to put these principles into practice is to create a personal code of ethics. Write down the values that are important to you and the principles you want to live by. This code can serve as a guide when you're faced with difficult financial decisions. For example, if honesty is one of your core values, then returning that extra change is a no-brainer. If fairness is important to you, then you might turn down that high-paying job with unethical practices in favor of a lower-paying one that aligns with your values.

REMEMBER:

Making ethical financial choices might seem challenging, but it's all about staying true to your values and principles. By being honest, fair, accountable, and transparent, you can navigate the financial world with integrity and confidence. Remember, it's not just about making the right choices for yourself but also for others. Your ethical decisions can have a positive impact on your family, friends, and even the broader community. So next time you're faced with a financial dilemma, take a moment to reflect on your values and make a choice that aligns with your personal code of ethics.

9.2 FINANCIAL RESPONSIBILITY: UNDERSTANDING THE CONSEQUENCES

Repetitive here because it is so important. Picture this: you've just received your first paycheck from your part-time job, and the possibilities seem endless. But before you rush off to splurge on the latest tech, let's talk about what it means to be financially responsible. Financial responsibility isn't just a buzzword; it's a way of life that involves managing your money wisely, meeting financial obligations on time, and living within your means. Think of it as a roadmap to financial stability.

Managing money wisely means knowing where your money is coming from and where it's going. It's about creating a budget that helps you allocate funds for essentials, savings, and a bit of fun without overspending. Meeting financial obligations on time is crucial because it builds trust and keeps you out of trouble. Whether paying your phone bill, a loan installment, or repaying a friend, being punctual shows you're reliable. Living within your means is all about spending less than you earn. It might sound simple, but it's one of the hardest yet most rewarding habits to develop.

Now, let's talk about what happens when financial responsibility goes out the window. As I've stressed, accumulating debt is one of the most immediate consequences of poor financial management. Imagine maxing out your credit card on impulse buys, only to realize you can't pay it off. That debt doesn't just disappear; it grows with interest, making it harder to dig yourself out. Next comes the potential for legal issues. If you're unable to pay your debts, creditors might take legal action against you, leading to even more stress and financial strain. Then there's the matter of your credit score. A poor credit score can haunt you for years, affecting your ability to get loans, rent an apartment, or even get a job. Defaulting on a loan, for example, can have long-term repercussions. Not only will you face higher interest rates in the future, but you might also find it difficult to secure any form of credit. It's like trying to swim with a weight tied to your ankle—possible, but incredibly challenging.

So, how do you develop financial responsibility? You know the answer! Start by setting and adhering to a budget. It's your best tool for managing money wisely. Write down all your income sources and expenses, and allocate funds accordingly. Prioritize savings and emergency funds. Putting aside a little each month can build a safety net for unexpected expenses. Avoiding unnecessary debt is another crucial step. Before taking on any debt, ask yourself if it's really necessary. If it's not, steer clear. Instead, save up for what you want. This might take longer, but it's a healthier financial habit.

Let's look at some real-life stories. Take the example of Larry, a teen who learned financial responsibility the hard way. Larry got his first credit card and went on a spending spree, only to find himself buried in debt. It took years of stress, diligent budgeting, and disciplined saving to recover, but he did it. Now, he's financially stable and wiser for the experience. On the flip side, there's Sarah, who practiced financial discipline from a young age. She always saved a portion of her allowance and any money she earned from odd jobs. By the time she graduated high school, she had a substantial savings account, which helped her pay for college without taking on student loans. Freedom! Her early start in managing money wisely set her up for long-term success.

Financial responsibility is more than just a concept; it's a practice that can lead to a secure and fulfilling life. Whether you learn from mistakes or start with good habits, the key is to stay committed to managing your money wisely.

9.3 PROTECTING YOUR PERSONAL INFORMATION: FINANCIAL SECURITY

Ever had that gut-wrenching moment when you realize you might have lost your wallet? Now, imagine that feeling but amplified because it's not just cash and cards you're worried about—it's your entire financial identity at risk. Protecting your personal financial information is crucial because it helps prevent identity theft, avoid financial fraud, and ensure your privacy and security.

Think of your financial data as a treasure trove. If it falls into the wrong hands, the consequences can be devastating. Identity theft can lead to someone opening credit accounts in your name, racking up debt, and leaving you with the mess to clean up. Financial fraud, on the other hand, can drain your bank accounts and ruin your credit score, making it harder for you to secure loans or even rent an apartment in the future. Ensuring your privacy means keeping your personal information safe from prying eyes and potential thieves.

So, how can you safeguard your financial data? Start by using strong, unique passwords for all your financial accounts. Avoid using the same password across multiple sites, and make sure your passwords are a mix of letters, numbers, and symbols. Next, be diligent about shredding sensitive documents before discarding them. Bank statements, credit card bills, and any paperwork with personal information should be shredded to prevent dumpster divers from getting their hands on your data. When it comes to sharing information online, exercise extreme caution. Never share personal or financial details over email or unsecured websites. Always verify the authenticity of the site before entering any information. Public Wi-Fi might be convenient, but it's also a hotspot for hackers. Avoid accessing financial accounts or making transactions when connected to public networks.

If you find yourself a victim of a financial breach, swift action is crucial. Start by reporting the breach to authorities, such as the **Federal Trade Commission (FTC)** and your local police department. Next, monitor your credit reports for any suspicious activity. You now know that you're entitled to a free credit report from each of the three major credit bureaus once a year, so take advantage of this to keep an eye on your credit. If necessary, consider freezing your credit accounts. This prevents new accounts from being opened in your name without your permission. Contact your banks and creditors to inform them of the breach and follow their procedures for securing your accounts.

REMEMBER:

Financial security is about protecting your personal information from being compromised. It's about being proactive and vigilant, ensuring that your financial data remains safe and secure. By using strong passwords, shredding sensitive documents, and being cautious with online information, you can significantly reduce the risk of identity theft and financial fraud. Recognizing common scams and knowing how to respond to a breach are essential skills that will help you navigate the financial world with confidence. Stay alert, protect your information, and you'll be well on your way to financial security.

9.4 THE RIPPLE EFFECT: HOW YOUR FINANCIAL CHOICES IMPACT OTHERS

Your financial choices don't just affect you—they can impact your family, friends, and even the broader economy. For example, buying something expensive might mean asking your parents for extra cash later, which can strain relationships. Similarly, your spending habits can influence your friends, either pushing them to overspend or inspiring them to save.

By managing your money wisely, you help create financial stability for yourself and contribute to a healthier economy. It's about thinking long-term and considering how your choices affect those around you. Supporting businesses with ethical practices and making thoughtful decisions can create a positive ripple effect, benefiting everyone. So, when making financial decisions, remember—they're not just about today, but also about the future and the people around you.

9.5 GIVING BACK: USING MONEY FOR GOOD

Got your first paycheck? It's tempting to splurge on something fun, but think about setting aside a bit for something more meaningful. Philanthropy might sound like a big word, but it's really just about using your money to make the world a better place. When you donate to causes you care about, like animal welfare or helping kids, you're not just helping others—you're also growing as a person and feeling good about yourself.

Even as a teen, there are plenty of ways to give back. You can donate a little money, join a fundraising event, or volunteer your time. Each of these actions helps build a stronger community and teaches you important lessons about empathy and money management.

Giving back doesn't have to be overwhelming. Start by setting aside a small percentage of your money for donations. Even $20 a month adds up to $240 a year, making a real difference. Plus, making charity a part of your budget helps you prioritize what's important.

Philanthropy isn't just about kindness; it's an investment in a better world and your own growth. Whether you're donating, fundraising, or volunteering, every little bit counts. And in the process, you're not only helping others but also building good financial habits that will benefit you in the long run.

CHAPTER 10
PLANNING FOR YOUR FINANCIAL FUTURE

> " *"Someone's sitting in the shade today because someone planted a tree a long time ago."*
>
> WARREN BUFFETT

I've described your finances as a garden. You plant seeds, water them, and patiently wait for them to grow. You might not see results overnight, but with time and care, your garden flourishes. Your financial future works much the same way. By setting long-term financial goals, you're planting the seeds for a secure and prosperous future. These goals are more than just dreams; they're actionable plans that guide you toward financial success. Let's dig in and see how you can set yourself up for a bright financial future.

10.1 SETTING LONG-TERM FINANCIAL GOALS: PLANNING AHEAD

You might not think now is the time to think about long-term goals, especially when you're busy juggling school, friends, and maybe even a part-time job. But setting these goals now to navigate your financial life is crucial for several reasons. First, it ensures future financial security. Imagine never having to worry about unexpected expenses because you've got a cushion of savings. Sounds nice, right? By planning ahead, you can achieve the significant life milestones I've talked about. Second, it will provide peace of mind that comes from avoiding financial stress later in life.

To start, you need to identify your personal aspirations. Do you dream of traveling the world? Maybe you want to buy a house or retire comfortably. Whatever your goals, write them down. Next, estimate the financial requirements for each goal. How much money will you need to achieve these dreams? Research and put a number on it. For example, if you want to buy a house, look into current market prices and factor in additional costs like maintenance and insurance. Once you have a clear picture, set realistic timelines. Break these goals down into smaller, manageable steps. For instance, if you plan to save $20,000 for a down payment on a house in five years, you'll need to save $4,000 per year, or about $333 per month.

Patience and persistence are key when it comes to long-term goals. It's easy to get discouraged by setbacks, but remember, every small step counts. You might face unexpected expenses or changes in your financial situation, and that's okay. Adjust your goals as necessary and keep moving forward. Celebrate small milestones along the way. Did you save $1,000 toward your goal? That's worth celebrating!

Let's look at some real-life examples to see how others have successfully set and achieved their long-term financial goals. Take Mia, a teenager who dreamed of traveling the world during a gap year before college. She started by setting a goal to save $10,000 over two years. Mia took on a part-time job, cut back on unnecessary expenses, and set up an automatic savings plan. She also picked up freelance work during school breaks. By the time her gap year arrived, Mia had saved more than enough to fund her travels and even had a little extra for spontaneous adventures.

Another example is Nehemiah, a young adult who aimed to buy his first home by the age of 30. Nehemiah started planning in his early 20s. He researched the housing market, set a savings goal for the down payment, and created a detailed budget. He also invested a portion of his savings in low-risk mutual funds to grow his money faster. Despite facing a few setbacks, like unexpected medical bills, Nehemiah adjusted his plan and stayed committed. By the time he turned 30, Nehemiah not only had enough for the down payment but also built a strong credit history, which helped him secure a favorable mortgage rate.

Setting long-term financial goals is not just about saving money; you're building a foundation for a life that's free from financial stress and full of opportunities. So start now!

10.2 REFLECTIVE EXERCISE: SETTING YOUR LONG-TERM FINANCIAL GOALS

Reflect on and execute the following steps and write down your plan (and **the Bonus Chapter will really help here**). Keep it somewhere visible to remind yourself of your goals and the steps you're taking to achieve them. Remember, the path to financial success is a marathon, not a sprint. Stay patient, stay persistent, and enjoy the journey.

1. **Identify Your Goals:** Write down three major financial goals you want to achieve in the next 5-10 years.
   ◦ Example: Save $15,000 for a car, build a $10,000 emergency fund, or save $30,000 for college.
2. **Estimate Financial Requirements:** Research and note down how much money you'll need for each goal.
   ◦ Example: Research car prices, tuition fees, or typical emergency fund amounts.
3. **Set Realistic Timelines:** Break down each goal into smaller, manageable steps.
   ◦ Example: Saving $15,000 for a car in 3 years means saving $5,000 per year or about $417 per month.
4. **Plan for Setbacks:** Think about potential obstacles and how you might overcome them.
   ◦ Example: If you face unexpected expenses, adjust your savings plan but stay committed to your goals.
5. **Celebrate Milestones:** Identify small milestones to celebrate along the way.
   ◦ Example: Each time you save $1,000, treat yourself to a small reward for your efforts and success.

10.3 PREPARING FOR COLLEGE: FINANCIAL TIPS FOR STUDENTS

It's easy to get caught up in the excitement of college life—new friends, new experiences, and a fresh start. But before you pack your bags, let's talk about something equally important: how to manage the financial side of things. Early college financial planning is important, reducing your reliance on student loans and easing financial stress during your college years. Imagine starting your adult life without being buried under a mountain of debt. Sounds good, right?

One of the first steps in planning for college expenses is opening a 529 college savings plan. This type of account offers tax advantages, making it an effective way to save for higher education. Contributions grow tax-free, and withdrawals for qualified education expenses are also tax-free. It's like giving your money a little boost to help it grow faster. If you start early, even small contributions can add up over time, thanks to compound interest. So, talk to your parents or guardians about setting one up if they haven't already.

Another practical tip for saving for college is setting aside a portion of your part-time job earnings. Yes, it's tempting to spend it all on the latest tech or nights out with friends, but think long-term. Allocating even a small percentage of your earnings to a college fund can make a significant difference. Plus, it builds good saving habits that will serve you well beyond college. To make this easier, consider setting up an automatic transfer to your savings account. That way, you won't even miss the money because it never hits your spending account.

Don't forget about scholarships and grants. These are essentially free money that you don't have to pay back, so take advantage of them. Start by researching available scholarships early and make a list of those you're eligible for. Websites like Fastweb and the College Board's Scholarship Search are great resources. Also, don't overlook smaller, local scholarships; they might not offer as much as national ones, but every little bit helps. Applying for scholarships can be time-consuming, but think of it as a part-time job that pays off big time.

When it comes to budgeting for college expenses, you'll need to account for more than just tuition and fees. Books and supplies can add up quickly, so it's essential to include them in your budget. Look for used textbooks or consider renting them to save money.

And let's not forget living expenses. Whether you're staying on campus or renting an apartment, you'll need to budget for housing, food, and other necessities. Create a detailed budget that breaks down all these costs. Make sure to include a buffer for unexpected expenses because, let's face it, life is unpredictable.

Managing money during college can be challenging, but there are strategies to make it easier. First, take advantage of student discounts. Many businesses offer discounts to students, so always ask if one is available. From software subscriptions to movie tickets, these discounts can add up to significant savings over time. Another tip is to find part-time work or campus jobs. Not only do these provide a steady income, but they also offer valuable work experience that can boost your resume. Look for jobs that align with your field of study or interests to make the most of your time.

By now, I know you've got my message on credit card debt. If you do use a credit card, make sure to pay off the balance in full each month to avoid interest charges. Better yet, stick to a debit card (no credit) or cash to keep your spending in check. Create a monthly budget and track your expenses to ensure you're staying within your limits. There are plenty of budgeting apps that can help you manage your money and keep track of your spending.

REMEMBER:

College is a time for learning and growth, not financial stress. By planning ahead and using these tips, you can focus on your studies and enjoy your college experience without constantly worrying about money. So, start saving early, apply for scholarships, create a budget, and manage your expenses wisely. You've got this!

10.4 YOUR FINANCIAL ROADMAP: CREATING A PLAN FOR THE FUTURE

Creating a financial roadmap is a lot like planning a road trip. It's a comprehensive plan that helps you navigate your financial life, ensuring you reach your destinations without running out of gas—or cash—along the way.

First, let's talk about the key components of a comprehensive financial roadmap. Much of this will sound familiar, but it's important to reinforce. Think of it as your financial toolkit. You'll need to consider your income sources and projections. Where is your money coming from now, and where might it come from in the future? This includes your job, side hustles, investments, or any other sources of income. Next, savings and investment strategies are crucial. How will you save money for future goals, and where will you invest to grow your wealth? This could involve setting up a savings account, investing in stocks, or even starting a retirement fund. Debt management plans are also a vital part of your roadmap. If you have any debt, how will you pay it off? What's your strategy to avoid accumulating more debt? Lastly, don't forget insurance and risk management. This includes health insurance, car insurance, and even life insurance to protect against unexpected events.

Now, let's break down the steps to create your personalized financial roadmap. Start by assessing your current financial situation. Take a good, hard look at your income, expenses, savings, and any debt you have. It's a necessary step to understand where you stand. Once you have a clear picture, set both short-term and long-term financial goals. Short-term goals might include saving for a new laptop or paying off a small credit card debt. Long-term goals could be buying a house, starting a business, or saving for retirement. Develop actionable steps to achieve these goals. For example, if your goal is to save $5,000 in a year, break it down into saving a specific amount each month. Create a budget that aligns with these steps, ensuring you're setting aside money for your goals each month.

Regular financial reviews are crucial to ensure you stay on track. Life is unpredictable, and your financial situation can change. Maybe you get a raise, or perhaps an unexpected expense pops up. Periodically reassessing and adjusting your financial roadmap helps you adapt to these changes. Set a reminder for annual financial check-ups. During these check-ups, review your income, expenses, savings, and goals. Are you on track? Do you need to adjust your budget or savings plan? Reevaluating your goals and timelines ensures they remain realistic and achievable.

Consider the story of Emma, a young professional planning for retirement. Emma started by assessing her current financial situation and realized she needed to increase her savings. She set a long-term goal to retire by 60 with a comfortable nest egg. Emma developed a plan to save a portion of her income each month and invested in a diversified portfolio of stocks and bonds. She also set up an emergency fund to cover unexpected expenses. Each year, Emma reviewed her financial roadmap, adjusting her savings plan and investment strategies as needed. By staying committed and regularly reviewing her plan, Emma is well on her way to achieving her retirement goal.

Another example is the Martinez family, who created a financial roadmap for home ownership. They started by setting a goal to buy a house within five years. The family assessed their current financial situation, including their income, expenses, and savings. They realized they needed to cut back on unnecessary expenses and increase their savings. They created a budget that allowed them to save a specific amount each month for a down payment.

The Martinez family also focused on paying off their existing debt to improve their credit score. Each year, they reviewed their financial roadmap, adjusting their savings plan and budget as needed. By staying committed and regularly reviewing their plan, the Martinez family is on track to achieve their goal of home ownership.

Creating a financial roadmap requires careful planning, regular reviews, and adjustments along the way. But with a clear plan, you can navigate your financial life with confidence, ensuring you reach your destinations without running out of gas or cash. So, grab a pen, map out your financial goals, and start planning your future today. Your financial success is just a roadmap away.

REMEMBER:

By mapping out your financial goals and creating a comprehensive plan, you set yourself up for a future of financial stability and success. Regular reviews and adjustments ensure you stay on track, no matter what life throws your way. Up next, we'll explore how to make the most of your financial journey, from investing wisely to managing your money with confidence.

CONCLUSION

Well, here we are at the end of our financial journey together. Congratulations! Remember when we started this book? We talked about the basics of financial literacy and why it's crucial for teens and supportive parents alike. Knowing how to manage money isn't just about balancing a checkbook or saving for a rainy day—it's about setting yourself up for a life where you're in control of your finances, not the other way around.

Throughout this book, we've explored a lot, from understanding the basics of budgeting and saving to diving into more complex topics like investing and smart spending. We've walked through real-life scenarios and provided practical exercises to help you apply what you've learned. The goal was to make these concepts not just informative but also engaging and relatable. After all, managing money should feel empowering, not overwhelming.

Let's quickly recap some of the main points:

1. **Budgeting Skills:** You learned how to create and maintain a budget, track your spending, and adjust as needed. Budgeting is your financial game plan, helping you allocate your resources wisely.

2. **Saving Money:** We discussed the importance of saving, building an emergency fund, and setting both short-term and long-term savings goals. Saving money is like planting seeds for your financial future.

3. **Earning Money:** Whether through part-time jobs, side hustles, or even starting your own business, we covered various ways you can earn money as a teen. Earning your own money teaches valuable life skills and gives you financial independence.

4. **Banking Basics:** Opening your first bank account, understanding bank statements, and using ATMs and online banking safely were all part of this chapter. These are the foundational skills for managing your money.

5. **Credit and Debt Management:** We talked about the importance of building good credit, understanding credit scores, and strategies to avoid and manage debt. Good credit can open doors to many opportunities, while poor credit can close them.

6. **Investing:** We introduced the basics of investing, different types of investments, and the power of compound interest. Investing wisely can grow your money over time and set you up for long-term financial success.

7. **Financial Responsibility and Ethics:** Making ethical financial choices and understanding the ripple effect of those choices can positively impact your life and those around you. Financial responsibility is about more than

just money—it's about integrity and making thoughtful decisions.

Key Takeaways:

- **Financial literacy is a lifelong journey.** The earlier you start, the better off you'll be.
- **Budgeting, saving, and earning money** are fundamental skills that will serve you well throughout your life.
- **Understanding and managing credit and debt** is crucial for financial health.
- **Investing is a powerful tool for building wealth,** but it requires knowledge and discipline.
- **Ethical financial decisions and responsibility** can create a positive impact not just for you but for your community.

Now, here's my call to action for you: **Take what you've learned and put it into practice.** Start small if you need to. Create a budget, open that savings account, or even start researching investments. Share what you've learned with your friends and family. Financial literacy is like a superpower—the more people who have it, the stronger we all become.

As you move forward, remember to be patient with yourself. Financial management is a skill that takes time to develop. **Celebrate your small wins** and learn from your mistakes. Don't be afraid to seek advice when you need it. Whether it's from a parent, a teacher, or a financial advisor, there's always someone who can help you navigate your financial journey.

Lastly, know that you're not alone in this. I wrote this book because I believe in your potential to achieve financial independence and thrive. I'm passionate about helping teens and supportive parents overcome financial challenges because I know the impact it can have on your future. By taking control of your finances now, you're setting yourself up for a life of opportunities and security.

So, go out there and make your financial dreams a reality. You've got the knowledge, the tools, and the support to succeed. And remember, **every step you take, no matter how small, brings you closer to your goals.** Keep learning, keep growing, and most importantly, keep believing in yourself.

But before you go...

Take a look at the next chapter, a **Bonus Chapter** on using **AI (Artificial Intelligence)** to accelerate your understanding of all that you've learned, and make your money-related actions easier and more effective.

Also, don't forget to use the **Exercise Workbook** that reinforces everything this book has taught you. You can access it at this link:

https://www.playapublishers.com/smart-money-for-teens-workbook

Thank you for letting me be a part of your financial journey. Here's to your future success and financial freedom. **You've got this!**

BONUS CHAPTER: LEVERAGING AI FOR FINANCIAL SUCCESS: HOW CHATGPT CAN HELP TEENS MANAGE MONEY, SIDE HUSTLES, AND TIME

F irst for parents. Why am I including this Bonus Chapter? Simple. AI is not just a passing trend; it is a transformative force that is reshaping industries and redefining how we approach daily tasks. Embracing AI today means positioning your teen at the forefront of tomorrow's innovations—it's an essential step forward as AI continues to integrate deeper into every aspect of our lives.

In a world where technology is advancing at lightning speed, and as you begin your journey into personal finance, the tools available to manage your finances are more powerful and accessible than ever. Among these tools is ChatGPT, an AI developed by OpenAI that can assist you in various aspects of your financial journey— from managing your money and side hustles to preparing for college and optimizing your time, essentially becoming your personal assistant. This chapter explores how ChatGPT can be your secret weapon in navigating the often-complex world of personal finance, helping you stand out and succeed in ways you may not have imagined. But note! AI is still new and developing. And is known to maker errors. So check your work!

MASTERING PERSONAL FINANCES WITH CHATGPT

We've gone into detail about the importance of the building blocks of personal financial management. ChatGPT can be your guide in this crucial area, offering personalized advice and strategies that are easy to implement.

- **Creating a Budget**: ChatGPT can help you design a budget tailored to your specific needs and goals. Whether you're earning an allowance, working a part-time job, or managing gift money, ChatGPT can suggest how to allocate your funds for spending, saving, and investing.
- **Tracking Expenses**: Keeping track of where your money goes can be tricky, but ChatGPT can help you monitor your expenses, identify patterns, and suggest ways to cut unnecessary costs. This feature is particularly useful for teens who are just starting to take charge of their finances.
- **Learning Financial Concepts**: Still not sure what compound interest is or how credit works? ChatGPT can break down complex financial concepts into simple, understandable terms, ensuring you build a solid foundation of financial literacy.

AI FOR FINANCIAL FORECASTING AND FUTURE PLANNING

Once you've established a basic understanding of your financial situation, ChatGPT can help you simulate different financial scenarios and forecast how your savings and spending decisions will impact your future.

- **Simulating Financial Scenarios**: Let's say you want to know what happens if you save an extra $50 a month or invest your allowance in a savings account with compound interest. ChatGPT can calculate how these small changes will affect your future savings. It can even help you understand long-term financial growth through simple simulations, showing the power of small, consistent actions over time.

Example:

"ChatGPT, what happens if I save $100 every month for five years at 5% interest?"

ChatGPT could show the user how their savings grow and explain the role compound interest plays in their future.

By using AI for forecasting, you gain a clear understanding of how today's choices shape your financial future.

EXPLORING AND MANAGING SIDE HUSTLES WITH AI

The rise of the gig economy has opened up countless opportunities for teens to earn money outside of traditional part-time jobs. Whether you're passionate about a particular hobby or just looking to make some extra cash, ChatGPT can help you explore and manage side hustles effectively.

- **Finding the Right Hustle**: ChatGPT can suggest side hustles based on your interests, skills, and available time. Whether it's freelance work, online tutoring, or selling crafts, ChatGPT can help you identify opportunities that align with your goals.

- **Business Advice**: Once you've chosen a side hustle, ChatGPT can offer advice on how to get started, from setting up an online presence to managing client relationships. It can also help you navigate the basics of running a small business, such as pricing your services or products and keeping track of earnings and expenses.
- **Balancing Work and Life**: Managing a side hustle alongside school and extracurricular activities can be challenging. ChatGPT can help you create a schedule that allows you to balance your commitments without burning out, ensuring that your side hustle remains enjoyable and profitable.

AI IN NEGOTIATION AND DECISION-MAKING

Financial literacy is crucial, but knowing how to make informed decisions and negotiate in financial matters is just as important. ChatGPT can act as a decision-making assistant, guiding you through tough financial choices.

- **Decision-Making Support**: Whether you're negotiating for a raise at your part-time job or trying to decide between two different loan offers, ChatGPT can provide tips and strategies to help you make the best decision. By breaking down pros and cons or offering negotiation advice, ChatGPT helps you navigate tricky financial decisions with confidence.

Example:

"ChatGPT, how do I negotiate a higher rate for my side hustle?"

ChatGPT can give tips on presenting value, researching market rates, and confidently asking for a fair price.

With AI, you can approach financial decisions with clarity and informed confidence.

PREPARING FINANCIALLY FOR COLLEGE

College is one of the most significant financial investments you and your parents will make, and preparing for it can be daunting. However, with the help of ChatGPT, you can approach this challenge with confidence and clarity.

- **Scholarships and Grants**: ChatGPT can help you search for scholarships and grants that match your profile, potentially saving you thousands of dollars in tuition. It can also provide tips on how to craft compelling scholarship applications.
- **Budgeting for College**: College life comes with its own set of financial responsibilities. ChatGPT can assist you in creating a budget that accounts for tuition, books, living expenses, and social activities. It can also suggest ways to save money, such as buying used textbooks or finding affordable meal plans.
- **Understanding Loans**: If student loans are part of your college financing plan, ChatGPT can explain the different types of loans available, the terms you need to be aware of, and strategies for minimizing debt. This knowledge will empower you to make informed decisions and avoid common pitfalls associated with borrowing for education.

MAXIMIZING PRODUCTIVITY AND TIME MANAGEMENT

Time management is a crucial skill, especially when you're juggling school, extracurricular activities, a side hustle, and college prep. ChatGPT can help you optimize your time and increase your productivity.

- **Creating a Schedule**: ChatGPT can generate customized schedules that align with your daily routines and responsibilities. By helping you prioritize tasks, it ensures that you stay on top of your commitments while still having time for relaxation and socializing.
- **Setting Achievable Goals**: Goal setting is an essential part of personal growth, and ChatGPT can guide you in setting SMART goals—Specific, Measurable, Achievable, Relevant, and Time-bound—for your finances, academics, and personal life. It can also help you track your progress and adjust your plans as needed.
- **Boosting Focus and Efficiency**: Struggling to stay focused? ChatGPT can provide tips on how to improve concentration and efficiency. Whether it's suggesting productivity techniques, like the Pomodoro Technique (which uses a kitchen timer!), or helping you minimize distractions, ChatGPT is a valuable tool in your quest to make the most of your time.

AI FOR TAX PREP AND FILING

For teens starting to earn money, tax preparation can be a daunting task. ChatGPT can simplify tax-related questions and help you understand your obligations when you start earning income.

- **Tax Guidance**: ChatGPT can explain the basics of tax filing, from thresholds to deductions, giving you a clearer understanding of when and how to file taxes.

Example:

"ChatGPT, do I need to file taxes if I made $2,000 this year?"

ChatGPT could guide you through understanding thresholds and possible deductions that may apply.

With this guidance, you'll feel more confident and prepared when tax season rolls around.

LEVERAGING AI FOR SETTING UP AUTOMATED FINANCIAL TOOLS

One of the most powerful ways to take control of your financial future is by setting up automated systems for savings and payments. ChatGPT can help you get started by offering tips on how to automate key financial tasks.

- **Automation Setup**: Whether it's setting up automatic savings transfers or scheduling bill payments, ChatGPT can help you automate parts of your financial life to stay consistent with your goals.

Example:

"ChatGPT, how do I set up automatic transfers to my savings account?"

ChatGPT could walk you through the steps specific to your bank or service.

Automation helps ensure you stick to your financial goals effortlessly.

RESPONSIBLE AI USAGE AND DATA PRIVACY

While AI is incredibly useful, it's essential to use it responsibly. As a final point, it's important to emphasize the role of data privacy and security when leveraging AI in your financial journey.

- **AI Privacy and Security**: Always be aware of how your data is being used by the apps and platforms you interact with. ChatGPT can remind you to check privacy settings and use secure passwords, helping protect your financial information from breaches or misuse.

By staying mindful of security, you ensure that you're using AI safely and responsibly.

NARRATIVE SCENARIO: BRIAN'S JOURNEY WITH AI

Meet Brian Thompson, a 16-year-old high school junior from Cleveland, Ohio. Brian is a well-rounded student with a packed schedule. He's not only a dedicated student with a 3.0 GPA but also a star athlete on his school's basketball team, sings in the church choir, is an active member of the Boy Scouts, and volunteers regularly at his church. Despite his busy life, Brian has big dreams: he wants to save for college, start a side hustle, improve his time management skills, and be fully prepared for his future. Brian is excited about the potential of AI, especially ChatGPT, to help him achieve these goals.

MANAGING PERSONAL FINANCES

One evening after basketball practice, Brian sits down at his desk, feeling a bit overwhelmed by his financial responsibilities. He's been thinking about saving for college but isn't sure where to start. He pulls out his phone and opens up ChatGPT, which he recently heard about from a friend who used it to help with budgeting. He types, "Hey ChatGPT, I need help creating a budget."

ChatGPT responds almost instantly, asking Brian a few questions about his income, expenses, and financial goals. Brian explains that he earns money from a part-time job at a local grocery store and occasionally receives money for chores at home. His expenses include buying lunch at school, contributing to his phone bill, and setting aside some money for outings with friends.

ChatGPT analyzes the information and suggests a budget break-down: 50% of his income should go toward savings for college, 30% toward necessary expenses, and 20% toward personal spending. It even provides tips on how to reduce unnecessary spending, like packing lunch a few days a week to save money. Feeling more in control, Brian sets up automatic transfers to ensure his savings grow consistently.

EXPLORING A SIDE HUSTLE

Inspired by his success with budgeting, Brian decides to explore the idea of starting a side hustle. He's always been good at math and enjoys helping his classmates with their homework, so he thinks tutoring might be a good way to earn some extra money. "ChatGPT, what are some good side hustles for someone like me?" Brian asks.

ChatGPT suggests several options, including online tutoring, free-lance graphic design, and even selling homemade crafts. Intrigued by the tutoring idea, Brian asks for more details. ChatGPT walks him through the process: setting up an online profile on a tutoring platform, determining a fair hourly rate, and marketing his services to potential clients. It even offers negotiation tips to ensure Brian is confident asking for fair pay.

To ensure balance, ChatGPT helps Brian organize his schedule, reminding him not to overload himself. Excited, Brian sets up his tutoring profile that evening, following ChatGPT's step-by-step guidance. Within a week, he lands his first client—a freshman struggling with algebra. Not only is Brian earning extra money, but he's also gaining valuable experience managing his own small business.

PREPARING FINANCIALLY FOR COLLEGE

With his new side hustle and budgeting plan in place, Brian starts thinking more seriously about college. He knows he'll need financial aid and is determined to avoid taking on too much debt. He asks ChatGPT for help in finding scholarships and planning his college finances. "ChatGPT, how can I start preparing financially for college?"

ChatGPT begins by suggesting a list of scholarships Brian might qualify for, including ones specifically for student-athletes and those involved in community service. It offers advice on crafting compelling scholarship applications and even helps Brian outline his essay.

Additionally, ChatGPT helps Brian create a college budget. It estimates costs for tuition, room and board, books, and other expenses based on the universities Brian is interested in. The AI suggests ways to save money, such as applying for work-study programs and renting textbooks instead of buying them. It also explains different types of student loans, ensuring Brian fully understands the terms before making decisions about borrowing.

With ChatGPT's guidance, Brian feels confident about his financial future. He begins applying for scholarships with the AI's support, knowing he's doing everything he can to prepare for college.

OPTIMIZING TIME MANAGEMENT

With so many activities on his plate, time management is a constant challenge for Brian. He's got schoolwork, basketball practice, choir rehearsals, scouting activities, church volunteering, and now a tutoring side hustle to juggle. Feeling particularly stressed one Sunday evening, Brian asks ChatGPT for help. "ChatGPT, I need help managing my time better. My schedule is really hectic."

ChatGPT asks Brian to list all of his commitments and how much time each requires. After gathering the details, ChatGPT creates a weekly schedule that maximizes Brian's time. It suggests specific blocks for studying, practicing, tutoring, and relaxation. The AI also introduces Brian to the Pomodoro Technique—a method of working in focused intervals with short breaks—which helps him stay productive during study sessions.

ChatGPT sets reminders for important deadlines and events, ensuring Brian never misses basketball practice or choir rehearsal. With the AI-generated schedule, Brian feels less stressed and more in control of his time. He even has more time for his friends and family.

LEARNING FINANCIAL FORECASTING AND AUTOMATING FINANCIAL TASKS

As Brian grows more comfortable with AI, he decides to take things further. "ChatGPT, what would happen if I increased my monthly savings for college?" he asks.

ChatGPT simulates a financial scenario, showing Brian how much more he could save by adjusting his monthly contributions. It explains how small changes, compounded over time, could significantly increase his college fund. This motivates Brian to tweak his budget and boost his savings.

Additionally, ChatGPT guides Brian through setting up automated transfers for his savings and bill payments. Now, each month, part of his paycheck automatically goes into his college fund, and his phone bill gets paid on time—no stress, no missed payments.

NAVIGATING TAXES AND RESPONSIBLE AI USE

As Brian's tutoring business grows, he starts wondering about taxes. "ChatGPT, do I need to file taxes if I made $2,500 from tutoring?" he asks.

ChatGPT explains the basics of income thresholds and tax obligations, helping Brian understand when and how he needs to report his earnings. It even provides tips on tracking his expenses to ensure he maximizes his deductions. Additionally, ChatGPT reminds Brian to always use secure passwords and be mindful of data privacy as he interacts with financial platforms and apps, reinforcing the importance of security in the digital age.

BRIAN'S FUTURE WITH AI

As Brian continues to use ChatGPT, he realizes how powerful AI can be in helping him manage his life. Whether it's organizing his finances, growing his side hustle, preparing for college, or optimizing his time, ChatGPT is always there to provide support and guidance.

One day, while talking to his friends about his experiences, Brian says, "I never thought an AI could help me so much. It's like having a personal coach for everything—money, school, time management—you name it."

His friends are impressed, and a few decide to try using ChatGPT themselves. Brian smiles, knowing he's found a secret weapon that's helping him not just keep up with his busy life but excel in it.

As Brian looks toward the future, he feels more prepared than ever. With AI by his side, he's confident he can achieve his goals—whether it's getting into his dream college, growing his tutoring business, or simply managing his packed schedule. And the best part? He's just getting started.

THE FUTURE OF AI IN PERSONAL FINANCE

While AI may seem novel or even a bit intimidating at first, it is quickly becoming an essential tool in various aspects of life, including personal finance. For teens like Brian, AI presents a unique opportunity to manage money, explore entrepreneurial ventures, and prepare for the future with ease and confidence. ChatGPT is more than just a tool—it's a partner in success, providing personalized advice and support whenever you need it.

Conclusion

Integrating AI into your financial journey can significantly impact how you manage your money, explore new income opportunities, prepare for college, and organize your time. ChatGPT is more than just a tool—it's your personal financial coach, helping you navigate each step of the way. The habits and knowledge you establish now will shape your financial future.

By embracing the power of AI early, you set yourself apart. Let ChatGPT guide you toward smarter, more informed decisions, giving you the confidence to achieve your goals and thrive.

REPRESENTATIVE REFERENCES

Why financial literacy is an important life skill for youths https://www.rbcwealthmanagement.com/en-ca/insights/why-financial-literacy-is-an-important-life-skill-for-youths

20 financial words parents should explain to their kids https://www.gohenry.com/uk/blog/financial-education/20-financial-words-parents-should-explain-to-their-kids

Important Financial Goals for Teens | Family Finance https://money.usnews.com/money/personal-finance/family-finance/articles/important-financial-goals-for-teens

The Psychology of Spending: Understanding Your Money ... https://myfirecu.org/the-psychology-of-spending-understanding-your-money-mindset/

Budgeting for Teens: What You Need to Know https://www.thebalancemoney.com/how-to-teach-your-teen-about-budgeting-4160105

Best Budgeting Apps for Teens (I Tried Them All) https://www.kidsmoney.org/teens/budgeting/apps/

Sample Monthly Budget for Teens https://fndusa.org/wp-content/uploads/2015/06/SampleBudgetforTeens.pdf

Common financial problems for teens & how to resolve them https://www.gohenry.com/us/blog/financial-education/common-financial-problems-for-teens-how-to-resolve-them

Teenagers and saving | Consumer Financial Protection Bureau https://www.consumerfinance.gov/consumer-tools/money-as-you-grow/teen-young-adult/explore-saving/#:~:text=Having%20money%20in%20a%20savings,rate%20in%20case%20of%20emergency.

How to Help Teens Harness the Power of Compound Interest https://www.firstalliancecu.com/blog/teach-teens-compound-interest

Emergency Funds Explained for Teens https://www.mydoh.ca/learn/money-101/building-credit/emergency-funds-explained-for-teens/

Setting Financial Goals: A Practical Guide for Teenagers https://www.azcentralcu.org/blog/financial-goals-for-teenagers/

Teen Jobs That Pay Well | Careers | U.S. News - Money https://money.usnews.com/careers/salaries-and-benefits/articles/teen-jobs-that-pay-well

Balancing High School and Part-Time Work - Big Future https://bigfuture.college

board.org/plan-for-college/stand-out-in-high-school/stay-motivated/balanc
ing-high-school-and-part-time-work

10 Successful Young Entrepreneurs https://www.investopedia.com/10-successful-
young-entrepreneurs-4773310

24 Ways Teens Can Make Money Online https://www.gohenry.com/us/blog/finan
cial-education/24-ways-teens-can-make-money-online

Best Teen Checking Accounts of 2024 https://www.businessinsider.com/personal-
finance/banking/best-teen-checking-accounts

How to Open a Bank Account: A Step-by-Step Guide https://rates.fm/banks/how-to-
open-a-bank-account-a-step-by-step-guide/

Why It Is Important to Do Monthly Bank Statement Reviews https://www.logixbank
ing.com/guides/why-it-is-important-to-do-monthly-bank-statement-reviews

10 Online & Mobile Security Tips - Better Money Habits https://bettermoneyhabits.
bankofamerica.com/en/privacy-security/online-security-privacy-tips

How to Teach Our Kids to be Frugal - The Journey At Home https://www.thejourney
athome.com/how-to-teach-our-kids-to-be-frugal/

TEENS – 10 TIPS ON SMART SPENDING https://www.td.com/content/dam/tdb/
document/pdf/personal-banking/teenssmartspendingtips-en.pdf

How to stop your teen from impulsive spending https://www.gohenry.com/uk/blog/
financial-education/how-to-stop-your-teen-from-impulsive-spending

Children, Adolescents, and Advertising | Pediatrics https://publications.aap.org/pedi
atrics/article/118/6/2563/69735/Children-Adolescents-and-Advertising

Credit Tips for Teens https://www.investopedia.com/credit-tips-for-teens-7152864

8 Ways to Help Your Teen Build Good Credit Now https://www.experian.com/blogs/
ask-experian/how-to-help-your-teen-build-credit/

Best College Student Credit Cards of August 2024 https://www.nerdwallet.com/best/
credit-cards/college-student

Paying Off Debt Strategies: Debt Snowball \u0026 More https://www.equifax.com/
personal/education/debt-management/articles/-/learn/paying-off-debt-
strategies/

Investing for Teens: What They Should Know https://www.investopedia.com/invest
ing-for-teens-7111843

Saving vs. Investing: Understanding the Key Differences https://www.investopedia.
com/articles/investing/022516/saving-vs-investing-understanding-key-
differences.asp

The Power of Compound Interest: Calculations and ... https://www.investopedia.com/
terms/c/compoundinterest.asp

7 Best Micro-Investing Apps for 2024 https://millennialmoneyman.com/micro-
investing/

Ethics In Finance - What It Is, Principles, Scope, Examples https://www.wallstreet mojo.com/ethics-in-finance/

7 Money Management Lessons for Teens https://www.fbfs.com/learning-center/4-lessons-to-teach-teens-about-financial-responsibility

8 Tips for Keeping Your Financial Information Secure https://creativeplanning.com/ insights/financial-planning/8-tips-for-keeping-your-financial-information-secure/

For Better or Worse, Your Decisions Matter | St. Louis Fed https://www.stlouisfed.org/ annual-report/2016/for-better-or-worse-your-decisions-matter

6 long term goals for teens to prepare for their future https://greenlight.com/learning-center/life-moments-and-milestones/long-term-goals-for-teens

Personal Finance 101: 13 Essential Tips for College Students https://post.edu/blog/ financial-tips-for-college-students/

12 Steps to Designing Your Financial Roadmap https://money.usnews.com/money/ personal-finance/slideshows/12-steps-to-designing-your-financial-roadmap

Success Stories of People Who Achieved Financial Freedom https://medium.com/be-open/success-stories-of-people-who-achieved-financial-freedom-d455358c0bf4

Cochran, J. (2023, March 9). *How can I use AI for budgeting and saving?* NerdWallet https://www.nerdwallet.com/article/banking/ask-a-nerd-how-can-i-use-ai-for-budgeting-and-saving

Chapman, T. (2023, March 27). *AI Could Help Manage Your Money—If You Can Trust It*

Money. https://money.com/ai-could-help-manage-money/

Royal Bank of Canada. (2023, April 15). *How Artificial Intelligence Can Help You Manage Your Personal Finance.* RBC Royal Bank

https://www.rbcroyalbank.com/en-ca/my-money-matters/money-academy/ banking-basics/money-mindset/how-artificial-intelligence-can-help-you-manage-your-personal-finances/

Made in United States
Orlando, FL
23 November 2024